THE OFFER OF PARADISE IN OUR LIFETIME

K.R. Davis

TEACH Services, Inc.
P U B L I S H I N G
www.TEACHServices.com • (800) 367-1844

World rights reserved. This book or any portion thereof may not be copied or reproduced in any form or manner whatever, except as provided by law, without the written permission of the publisher, except by a reviewer who may quote brief passages in a review.

The author assumes full responsibility for the accuracy of all facts and quotations as cited in this book. The opinions expressed in this book are the author's personal views and interpretations, and do not necessarily reflect those of the publisher.

This book is provided with the understanding that the publisher is not engaged in giving spiritual, legal, medical, or other professional advice. If authoritative advice is needed, the reader should seek the counsel of a competent professional.

Copyright © 2019 K.R. Davis
Copyright © 2019 TEACH Services, Inc.
ISBN-13: 978-1-4796-0865-2 (Paperback)
ISBN-13: 978-1-4796-0868-3 (ePub)
Library of Congress Control Number: 2018959166

All Scriptures, unless otherwise stated, are taken from the King James Version of the Holy Bible.

Scripture quotations marked NKJV are from the New King James Version®. Copyright © 1982 by Thomas Nelson. Used by permission. All rights reserved.

Scripture quotations marked NASB are from the New American Standard Bible®. Copyright © 1960, 1962, 1963, 1968, 1971, 1972, 1973, 1975, 1977, 1995 by The Lockman Foundation. Used by permission.

Scripture quotations marked NIV are taken from THE HOLY BIBLE, NEW INTERNATIONAL VERSION®, NIV® Copyright © 1973, 1978, 1984, 2011 by Biblica, Inc.® Used by permission. All rights reserved worldwide.

Scripture quotations marked HCSB® are taken from the Holman Christian Standard Bible®. Copyright © 1999, 2000, 2002, 2003, 2009 by Holman Bible Publishers. Used by permission. HCSB® is a federally register trademark of Holman Bible Publishers.

Published by

TEACH Services, Inc.
PUBLISHING
www.TEACHServices.com • (800) 367-1844

Being recently touched by the Holy Spirit, I struggle with the how Scripture is to be applied to our everyday life. We have evolved over 2000 plus years and I feel biblical applications should evolve also. The author has taken his knowledge of the Bible and applied them to today. I am very impressed with that. Thank you.
— *Charles Lewis, Physical Therapy Aide/Materials Technician*

I believe it opens our eyes more to how the prophecies of God's word and of the Spirit of Prophecy are all lining up very accurately and it is a solemn reminder of just how close to the brink of eternity we truly are. It also contains precious reminders of how God's children will be strengthened for the coming conflict and will rise above the storms/waves of opposition, filled with peace from God which passes all understanding. I also admire the emphasis put on beholding Christ to the level of hearing His voice in our daily lives and living the life of Godliness in a godless world. How true that we must be so connected to and in tune with Christ that we may be partakers of God's special outpouring without measure, and soon afterward become partakers of His glory when Jesus returns. May this book help to open the eyes of many to the signs of the end and to serve as a guide to help people to know and understand what is going on all around us as well as behind the scenes.
— *Cherise Brown, Operator/Medical Records Department, Church Treasurer for Aurora 1st SDA Church*

The book, "The Offer of Paradise in Our Lifetime" lovingly presents the intimate relationship that God desires with His end time children. The book not only encourages us, but also reminds us of God's loving presence with us in our daily encounters. The author has a very realistic approach to the issues that are discussed. He is direct in imparting the knowledge and truths of the Bible and the spirit of prophecy to get the message clearly and quickly. It is simplistic and easy to comprehend but contains tremendous insights and profound biblical perspective. I highly recommended it to all who want to live their lives to the fullest and those who seek to find God and the real meaning and purpose of life. I would recommend this to all who are seeking the truth of God.
— *Tom Tupito, Pastor, Rocky Mountain Conference of the SDA Church*

Table of Contents

Introduction . . . . *ix*
Highest Ambition of Faith . . . .*xi*
Validity of an Earth Changeover—Is Straying of Earth Indefinite? . . . . . . *xii*
Previous "World Endings" . . . .*xiii*

Chapter 1
Knowing the Times **16**
Could People Possibly Affect the Timing of the End? 16
    Revealed Prophetic Fixed Time 17
    Unknown or Secret Fixed Time 21
        Accumulation of the Register of Sins 21
        Attitude of Imminent Expectation. 23
Heaven in Our Lifetime? 24
    Is There a Calling for His People to Shorten the Time? 24
    The Power to Delay or Expedite. 28
Hastening Objections 31
The Instrumental Closing Events Depend on Inside Signs
    Rather Than Outward Ones 34

Chapter 2
Holy Festivals Foretell and Typify the Restoration Journey. **36**
Preparing the Way. 36
    Rise of the Reformation out of which Emerges
        the Advent Movement. 39

    Remnant Reflecting the Character of Christ 40
    Proclaim the Gospel Until It Covers the Globe 41
Passover and First Fruits 43
Pentecost Shadow Fulfillment and the First
    of Three Bible Rains. 44
    Early Rain 45
    Dew and Small Rains 46
    Latter Rain 48

Chapter 3
Trumpets and Solemn Day of Atonement Shadow Fulfillments **51**
First Phase—Jesus in the Sanctuary Sends Seven
    Trumpeting Angels 53
Second Phase—Jesus in the Sanctuary for the Day of Atonement 56
    Early Advent Awakening—A Small-Scale Model 58
    Was All Judgment Finished at the Cross? 59
    Pre-advent Judgment Prepares the Bride for the Marriage 61
        First Wedding Parable—Matthew 25:1–13 64
        Second Wedding Parable—Luke 14:7–24 70
        Third Wedding Parable—Matt. 22:1–14 72
    The Personal Effect of This Judgment for Hastening Christ 77
    Restoration Level of Righteousness by Faith 79
        Abiding in Christ Level of Righteousness by Faith 84
        Communion Level of Righteousness of Faith 86
        The Greatest Work 96
    Christ Comes to the Soul's Door and Heaven's Temple Door 99
        The Soul's Door 100
        Heaven's Temple Door 102

Chapter 4
The Feast of Tabernacles Shadow Fulfillment **107**
Zechariah's Prophecy of the Latter Rain 112

Global Scale of Rains Compared—The Work of
    a Single Generation 114
Wedding Continues with Reception Supper. 119
Tabernacles of Revelation—The Loud Cry Draws
    the Nations to Jesus (See also chapter 8). 123
Now is the Time for Rain—The Dawning of Eternity. 125
Deepening Darkness of the Final Days Makes Brighter
    the Glory of God. 129
The Sealing Coincides with the Latter Rain. 136

Chapter 5
Hastening Window of Opportunity **139**
Historicist Basis. 139
On the Prophetic Timeline, When Did the Hastening
    Window of Opportunity Open?. 140
Is It Possible to Miss the Window of Opportunity?. 144
        Postponement of the Latter 1800s 145
Determining a Successful Window Closing 155
        The Other Window Alternative 157

Chapter 6
The Last Generation Identity **158**
They Were All with One Accord 158
The Elect of the Remnant 159
Simply a Majority Rules 161

Chapter 7
The Lord Draweth Nigh (James 5:7–9) **165**
Threshold Crossing in Flight History 165
Threshold Crossing Day. 172
        Accelerator 1—Hastening Prayers of the Elect. 172
        Accelerator 2—Faith Shaken, but Persevering 179

    Accelerator 3—Advancing Scripture Light 185
Opposition Awakens. 190
Popular Opposition Intensifies 193
Barrier Crossing Assurance 194

Chapter 8
Passing Through the Banquet Door, No Turning Back. **196**
Greatest Spiritual Awakening of All Time 197
Inflow of Thousands for the Harvest. 199
Great Changes in God's People. 201
Unrestrained Proclaiming of the Fall of Babylon 203
The Value of Miracles, Signs, and Wonders. 205
Open Persecution 206
Abrupt Turnover 209
Closing Time—Scanning the Eastern Sky 211

Conclusion *212*
We Are Well Able *214*
Bibliography *215*

Introduction

Along with creating masterpiece artwork, Leonardo da Vinci employed his genius in designing inventions far ahead of his time including a craft that could carry a person through the air. Apparently, he never made any attempts at fabrication, most likely due to the realization that even if a vessel launched into the air, it would not continue long in sustained flight without a propulsion force greater than mere, human-powered peddling or flapping of the wings.

It would be 400 more years before the first, controlled, manned flight—over the dunes of Kitty Hawk, North Carolina—gained official recognition. Since then advancements have proliferated, but beyond our moon there remains only hopeful contemplation.

One thing that da Vinci, the Wright brothers, and other flight enthusiasts before them carefully observed was the Creator's design for flight—"The way of an eagle in the air…" (Prov. 30:19). At times, the sight of a soaring bird ignites the imagination into longing for cosmic flight, especially in light of the galaxy-strewn realms recently observed. Although their brilliance beckons us, the vastness from even one star to another forces humanity to acknowledge that nothing less than the supernatural side of reality will suffice to get us off the ground for destinations to other worlds. Certainly, the divine design is in place, waiting for the right moment.

Although this journey will secure the restoration of humanity to eternal paradise and unlimited fellowship with our Maker, such a reunion, after thousands of years of disconnect, is unfortunately still as unwelcome by the world at large as was the first coming of Jesus. Yet the continuing decline of earth speaks of a new urgency for lifting the ship of mankind heavenward as the ultimate remedy to a greater degree than "putting out the fires" of human needs, as important as these may be. What could compare, though, with the restoration that will cure human woe for all time?

Many consider that His return depends on a cooperative effort between God and His people. In fact, there is a biblical passage in the form of instruction, as well as a promise that may be claimed by God's people who are living after the start of the "time of the end" over 170 years ago. If at least a united, believing elect will satisfy given conditions for receiving this promise, God will respond in power and suddenness, rewarding them with the return of Jesus in their lifetime. Why this hasn't happened for the previous four to six generations will be taken up shortly.

God details the process of fulfilling this promise through the representations of the Old Testament holy feast days, shadows "of things to come" (Col. 2: 17). Once the final feast fulfillment (Tabernacles) has begun, events cascade in favor of completing all the conditions required for the promise within that generation.

Jesus instructs His ancient and modern disciples to occupy until He comes (see Luke 19:13). The question follows, 'What kind of occupying did He intend?' To begin this answer, it depends on the age or generation in which the saints are living. For most of history, Scripture indicates that there was nothing believers could do about how soon He would appear. Therefore, occupying would have been a Christian life of hoping for the Second Coming and resurrection; but today, occupying includes helping in addition to hoping.

Like hope, many Scriptures emphasize waiting as a virtue of the saints, yet in respect of "present truth," others picture God as the One who is waiting. There's something that takes place among His people which results in much less of a wait for everybody, and then the heavenly announcement will be made that the time has arrived.

As represented in the Bible, the finishing movements for earth bring to mind the scene of an overhanging drift of snow on a mountain slope.

As long as everything above timberline remains quiet, several feet of snow remain fixed until the spring thaw; but a small vibration may be all it takes to bring the mass down to the valley. God has given advanced instruction and warning so all who take heed may remain out of harm's way. The end of humanity's captivity is not an arbitrary time, but dependent on a ripening combination of developments that could potentially begin an unstoppable cascade at any time by a single triggering event. However, as long as the population below remains unwarned, earth remains fallen, with mercy largely out of sight. Once a multitude has found safety, then total destruction of fallen earth will be allowed to commence. Only one small movement is left—a united acceptance of a simple invitation.

Highest Ambition of Faith

There are a couple of viewpoints held by Christians on the question of when this earth will come to an end as determined by spreading the gospel to the world. Many have no special concern about when this will happen. Others deeply yearn for the end and wonder how to direct their faith in helping it happen as expressed by this Christian writer:

> Success in any line demands a definite aim. He who would achieve true success in life must keep steadily in view the aim worthy of his endeavor. Such an aim is set before the youth of today. The heaven-appointed purpose of giving the gospel to the world *in this generation* is the noblest that can appeal to any human being. It opens a field of effort to everyone whose heart Christ has touched. (White, *Education*, p. 262, emphasis added)

Another statement by the same author goes a step further: "Their works show the character of their faith and testify to those around them that the coming of Christ is not to be *in this generation*. According to their faith will be their works. Their preparations are being made to remain in this world"

(White, *Testimonies for the Church*, Vol. 2, p. *196*, emphasis added). It would be quite rare to find anyone who would not like to wake up in heaven, and yet, with all the daily 'shock news,' there seems to be no hurry.

Validity of an Earth Changeover—
Is Straying of Earth Indefinite?

God has winked at ignorance, but then what (see Acts 17:30)? Will He continue to overlook the wayward tendencies of man for ages to come? For a given generation, is heaven only to be hoped for after death? Will God continually exercise patience until that point when earth can no longer support life? If earth's captivity was to go on with no clues of an ending in sight, then perhaps earth's inhabitants will be excused for becoming acclimated to mortality. In Acts 17:30, part of Paul's sermon to the Athenians, certain errors were overlooked during times of ignorance, "…but now [He] commandeth all men every where to repent." With the first coming of Christ came light that scattered ignorance, particularly in the area of the world's captivity to idolatry. Later, when the time of judgment arrives (see v. 31), the call of repentance is made regarding other truths lost to accumulated religious traditions over the centuries. A day appointed for judgment speaks of an inevitable, sudden finish line at some point.

Many people reason that it is preferable to wait until some remote point in the future. Understandably they want to allow sufficient time for more to be saved, letting the earth gradually melt down instead of end with a sudden, global destruction. The Scripture's response reveals that once sufficient enlightenment has encompassed the nations, there will necessarily be a decisive and abrupt conclusion to earth. Rather than giving everyone in the world a long time to decide until they pass to the grave, it is heaven's plan to develop conditions so that the populations of earth are brought to decision within a single generation. Otherwise, if time allows for more population turnover, then new rounds of gospel labor will be required. Plus, history notes that successive generations tend to decline spiritually after revival, time permitting.

What about the concern that sparsely few will be saved from the last generation? True, relative to the whole population, few find the narrow way, yet God has designed that when final destruction does occur, there will be saved an innumerable multitude. The end could not happen without this because in God's character, nothing else would so honor the Savior's sacrifice on Calvary but a vast population of living saints, in addition to the resurrected from the dead, welcoming His arrival. The idea is to avoid another near-total loss as when just a handful were saved at the first global destruction of Noah's day. Our time, as shown in prophecy, is ripe for the finishing movements to become a present reality.

> The Saviour's promise to His disciples is a promise to His church to the end of time. God did not design that His wonderful plan to redeem men should achieve only *insignificant results*. All who will go to work, trusting not in what they themselves can do, but in what God can do for and through them, will certainly realize the fulfillment of His promise. "Greater works than these shall ye do," He declares; "because I go unto My Father." (White, *The Desire of Ages*, p. 667, emphasis added)

Previous "World Endings"

Each of the ancient prophets spoke less for their own time than for ours, so that their prophesying is in force for us. "Now all these things happened unto them for ensamples: and they are written for our admonition, upon whom the ends of the world are come" (1 Corinthians 10:11). "Not unto themselves, but unto us they did minister the things, which are now reported unto you by them that have preached the gospel unto you with the Holy Ghost sent down from heaven; which things the angels desire to look into" (1 Peter 1:12). (White, *Selected Messages*, book 3, p. 338)

A few familiar examples of previous large and small-scale "world endings" serve as present-day object lessons. They came with suddenness, yet before these grave destructions came to pass, special interventions of God beyond the usual gave every member of the imperiled population the clear path of escape.

1. The global flood, prior to which Noah preached and built the ark for 120 years (Gen. 6–9)
2. Before the destruction of Sodom and Gomorrah, one resident remained as a godly example, ultimately being rescued by angels (Gen. 18, 19; 2 Peter 2:6–8)
3. Well aware of the divine signs and wonders that accompanied the children of God, Jericho and the other Caananite nations fell before the armies of Israel (Josh. 5:1; 6, 9–11)
4. The showdown at Mt. Carmel between the God of Elijah and Baal of Queen Jezebel and her priests, when fire fell from heaven and saved 7,000 Israelites from being overtaken by occult worship (1 Kings 18).
5. Christians in A.D. 70 remembered the instruction of Jesus. "And when ye shall see Jerusalem compassed with armies, then know that the desolation thereof is nigh. Then let them which are in Judaea flee to the mountains; and let them which are in the midst of it depart out; and let not them that are in the countries enter thereinto" (Luke 21:20, 21). Not a single believer was lost on that fateful day; the same outcome is assured at the last destruction.

As in the past, God will manifest supernatural intervention on behalf of His people during the closing scenes. The record of His past interventions also shows that God does nothing without revealing His secrets through His elect/prophets (see Amos 3:7). Also, at the end, there will be a scene of suddenness, but only after religious confusion has been quickly dispelled globally, leaving only two sides from which to choose before the "time of trouble, such as never was since there was a nation…" (Daniel 12:1). God's provisions being worked out for the brief window of the final curtain closing will assure that every soul has an abundance of advanced warning and opportunity. This is covered further in chapters 2 through 6 of this book.

Regarding direct acts of divine origin, philosophies have left multitudes in the dark through institutions of learning. Public educators are required to sustain that nothing in this world varies through supernatural means. This is the opposite of God's actual working, acting on people's thoughts and through continual providence. "A man's heart plans his way, But the Lord directs his steps" (Prov. 16:9, NKJV). Furthermore, Peter, in his second epistle, writes of those who remain willingly ignorant, which explains the apparent lack of sensing God's involvement in earth's affairs. In consequence of this, the day of the Lord, when it does come, will seem to be a "thief in the night" (3:5, 10). The will of man is the door that allows or prevents the benefit of God's guidance in the midst of relentless delusions.

> *The will of man is the door that allows or prevents the benefit of God's guidance in the midst of relentless delusions.*

Chapter 1

Knowing the Times

"What time is it?" and "What's the weather today?" are questions that pertain to making preparations for the day ahead. For the best answers, it helps to check reliable sources. Concerning future events, the Bible is the sole source.

"And that, knowing the time, that now it is high time to awake out of sleep: for now is our salvation nearer than when we believed" (Rom. 13:11). What if the "time" specified by Paul is especially intended for our time? The next verse provides the context, showing that this indeed was Paul's intention. "The night is far spent, the day is at hand: let us therefore cast off the works of darkness, and let us put on the armour of light." When one uses the expression "the day is at hand," it means, in a practical sense, a day that is imminent, within one's lifetime (our time). It should be faith-stirring if this is the case today—the idea of coming on the scene of history when knowing the time means *now is the time*.

Could People Possibly Affect the Timing of the End?

This could be ruled out if either one of these two options are presently active: prophetic fixed time or any fixed time that is not revealed.

Revealed Prophetic Fixed Time

The last question asked by His disciples before Jesus ascended was "Lord, wilt thou at this time restore again the kingdom to Israel" (Acts 1:6)? It is a similar to questions asked today by modern disciples. "How long until your kingdom comes to earth?" Jesus did not deny the validity of the question, but with His depth of wisdom, He replied to the first-generation Christians: "It is not for you to know the times or the seasons, which the Father hath put in his own power" (v. 7). Notice that He did not discourage this question from being asked at some point in the future. The authority over time that is normally attributed to the Lord doesn't rule out the sharing of this authority under the right conditions. Has God ever sought help from humans before over that which was ruled by His authority? Authority over time has been and will be granted in answer to prayer, as will be explored further ahead.

Moses was commanded by God to step aside so that Israel might be destroyed and replaced with a new nation to descend from Moses. He pleaded with God over this and the Lord had a change of heart (see Exod. 32:10–14).

The times and seasons established by the sun, moon, and earth had never been altered until the plea that Joshua made with God in His time of urgency. By a whole-hearted prayer of faith, Joshua authorized a cessation of the orbits of both the earth and moon, giving the impression that the sun and moon stood still. The Lord was pleased to perform this miracle, for no other reason than because His close friend Joshua requested it. The Lord could have given Joshua victory in a moment, as well as an ordinary day's time (see Josh.10:12–14).

The showbread, by command, was only for priests, but David and his men, in their famished state, were allowed to be fed by it (see 1 Sam. 21:6). Yes, God does have flexibility and will make exceptions on our behalf, often quite against normal expectations.

To the disciples—His elect—Jesus gave the answer which mattered most. Instead of "when," He gave the "how." The earthly reign of Jesus will advance nearer through this promise: "But ye shall receive power, after that the Holy Ghost is come upon you: and ye shall be witnesses unto me both in Jerusalem, and in all Judaea, and in Samaria, and unto the uttermost part of the earth" (Acts 1:8). This supplements Matthew 24:14: "And this gospel of the kingdom shall be preached in all the world for a witness unto all nations; and then shall the end come." Both passages declare our role in the finishing gospel witness. However, does this necessarily give us influence over the timing? Yes, it does, although Acts 1:7 reminds us that the ultimate authority over the timing is the Father. Other Scripture indicates that He bestows upon His people the privilege and honor of sharing a measure of His authority.

The word "times" in Acts 1:7, by Strong's definition of *chronos*, is "a space of time" or "interval." "Seasons" is translated from *kairos* and means "occasion, i.e. set or proper time." When Jesus gave His answer above, there were *many fixed prophetic times* yet to be fulfilled, such as the one to be fulfilled during Christ's life on earth: the seventy weeks (490 years) predicting the year of Christ's anointing through baptism in AD 27 and the end of probation for the Jewish nation in AD 34 (See *God Cares II*, p. 276, by Mervyn Maxwell, on the seventy weeks recorded in Dan. 9:24–27). Unlike the second advent, the first advent was anchored by a specific time and, therefore, offered no possibility of shortening it's timing.

Incidentally, if there is any question about whether the seventy weeks represents 490 literal years, taking each day to symbolize one year, there are two points to consider. First, the beginning of the seventieth week works out to be the very year of the anointing of Jesus in AD 27 through baptism, which counted from the year 457 BC, provided by the historical event recorded in Daniel 9 and Ezra 7:11–26. Three and a half years into the seventieth week (half a week) turned out to be the year Jesus gave His life in AD 31, as portrayed in Daniel 9:25–26.

Second, the subject of Daniel's prayer in chapter 9 was over the urgent issue of the soon-ending Old Testament time prophecy given in Jeremiah 29:10. Daniel lived near the ending of the seventy-year sentence of Israel's imprisonment under Babylon. These seventy years were based on redeeming seventy sabbatical years, the total years that the land had not rested from tilling, according to God's commandment. One year out of seven was the sabbatical year and seventy of them amounted to 490 years (see 2 Chron. 36:21). What the angel promised in Daniel 9:24 was essentially another 490 (seventy times seven) years of grace, equal to the previous 490 years of disobedience. Fittingly, Jesus chose this numerical expression (seventy times seven) to answer Peter's question on how many times to forgive a brother (see Matt, 18:22).

Many other fixed time prophecies, primarily in the books of Daniel and Revelation, have come and gone, the last of them ending in the year 1844, over 170 years ago (see Dan. 8:14).

The only possible, remaining, fixed time is one that is at best a rounded-off figure nearest to 6,000 years, when it is claimed that the world should end because 1,000 years after that is the seventh one, the millennium referred to in Revelation 20, 2 Peter 3:8, and Bible chronology. It is known as the Sabbath Millennium Theory, when earth will rest from 6,000 years of sin. It can be thought of as a general timeframe for the end, instead of a specific year. According to the latest Biblical chronology, starting with 4004 BC, the year of the fall of humanity, 6,000 more years brings us to 1997. If anything, we can say that earth is being given a generous extension.

"But of that day and hour knoweth no man, no, not the angels of heaven, but my Father only" (Matt. 24:36). Notice that this isn't about a set time that is not alterable, because the passage doesn't tell us that the date is immovable. It only speaks of the Father's exclusive foreknowledge of the date. At this stage, set times are no longer useful and perhaps even harmful, especially when it comes to a date for the end. Inevitably it would become a diverting focus, causing a neglect of the only secure preparation for the end—maintaining our devotional connection to Jesus.

History shows that the approach of a specific date for a "final" destruction does little to distinguish the genuine from the artificial among the followers of a date-setting message. Understandably, many would embrace external reforms fueled by excitement and fear. The story of Jonah is an object lesson. The Ninevites were given a fixed time—forty days—for the overthrow of their city; and not surprisingly, the whole city repented and was spared. However, was it a repentance of true conversion? Eventually Nineveh faltered and the city was quick to forget God and return to her old ways, so although destruction was postponed, unfortunately, it was not cancelled.

> *At this stage, set times are no longer useful and perhaps even harmful, especially when it comes to a date for the end. Inevitably it would become a diverting focus, causing a neglect of the only secure preparation for the end—maintaining our devotional connection to Jesus.*

In modern times, probably the most widely followed movement resulting from a date for the end was the Great Advent awakening of the 1840s. During the peak just prior to the finally settled date of October 22, 1844, hundreds of thousands attended meetings held across the United States. A contribution to the success of the revival was the biblical correctness of the date. When nothing happened on the earth that day, the Great awakening became the Great Disappointment, as symbolized by Revelation 10:8–10. The aftermath was a loss of faith by large numbers of the crowds who had gathered to meet Jesus in the air. As devastating as this appeared, God's purpose was working out—the gathering of an elect whose faith did not fail, who would continue to prayerfully study out the true event of October 22. Then they would "prophesy again" (v. 11).

Since 1844, the remaining prophecies are condition-based, and the Lord has graciously given them for the benefit of realizing His infinite power to read the future and safely guide us through it. The study of them removes all doubt about the expectation of the ultimate predicted event—the appearing of Jesus. Not every aspect of the time of His coming is avoided as though the time was not to occupy one's thought. On the contrary, since the timing is based on conditions rather than a specified time, then a great door of opportunity opens up to the privilege and potential for God's people to discover what roles they have in fulfilling prophecy, which in turn directly shortens the time. The saints then have a certain ownership for determining if His coming is within their generation or is passed on to the next.

Due to our condition-based era of history, the Lord's declaration in Acts 1:7 has been superseded. The times under the Father's power are now understood, leaving no remaining set times "which the Father hath put in His own power."

Unknown or Secret Fixed Time

This question then follows: Might the end be tied to an *unknown fixed time*, independent of human influence? Even with no further prophetic set times, does God set a time that is beyond any influence by the saints? If so, then does the Lord increasingly alert His people, moving them to carry out their roles with respect to such a time limit? The following is one consideration that has been raised.

Accumulation of the Register of Sins

What about the evidence of determining the day of God's wrath according to the mounting accumulation of sin? For example, Revelation 18:5 declares of end-time Babylon, "For her sins have reached unto heaven, and God hath remembered her iniquities." Another is the first global destruction by flood. In Genesis, the level of iniquity determined when the earth was ripe for judgment day. "The inhabitants of the antediluvian world ate and drank till the indulgence of depraved appetite knew no bounds, and they became so corrupt that God could bear with them no longer. They filled up the cup of their iniquity, and by a flood He cleansed the earth of its moral pollution." (White, *Signs of the Times*, December 1, 1914, par. 2). However, what determined the level of iniquity? Did this have something to do with the conviction brought on by the evidence and testimony given by Noah and his family while building the ark?

It turns out that God's measuring of the accumulation of sin and the appearing of Jesus are both dependent upon the cooperative roles of God's people. The recompense of destruction was withheld in mercy until their unanimous rejection of Noah's preaching and ship-building on their behalf for 120 years. They could neither plead ignorance or lack of opportunity to know their true condition before God. "By Faith Noah, being warned of God of things not seen as yet, moved with fear, prepared an ark to the saving of His house; *by the which he condemned the world*, and became heir of the righteousness which is by faith" (Heb. 11:7, emphasis added).

Abraham was told by God that the timing of Israel's release from Egypt depended on His mercy to the Amorites living in the Promised Land. "But in the fourth generation they shall come hither again: for the iniquity of the Amorites is not yet full" (Gen. 15:16). What makes iniquity reach this full level? Isn't this proportional to the level of light, warning, and instruction given by God and His commissioned people then and now? Gibeon, one of the cities of the Amorites, actually heeded the light concerning Israel, and they found mercy (see Josh. 9:1–9; 10:1, 2).

Commenting on Revelation 20:12, Ellen White wrote:

> There is an unerring register kept of all sins committed. All man's impiety, all his disobedience to Heaven's commands, are written in the books of heaven with unerring accuracy. The figures of guilt rapidly accumulate, yet the judgments of God are tempered with mercy, until the figures have reached their appointed limit. God bears long with the transgression of human beings, and *continues through His appointed agencies to present the gospel message, until the set time has come*. God bears with divine patience with the perversity of the wicked;

but He declares that He will visit their transgressions with a rod. He will at last permit the destructive agencies of Satan to bear sway to destroy (MS 17, 1906). (White, *The SDA Bible Commentary*, vol. 4, p. 1171, emphasis added)

Notice what is stated about the appointed limit. Overall, the quotation is about "the figures of guilt," a line that is based on a moral measure which, according to Matthew 24:14, is established by presenting the gospel to every people. It is a set time in terms of God's foreknowledge of when the gospel spread is globally complete. Therefore, both concepts—a timing based on 1) the people of God and 2) the full cup of iniquity—are applicable and compatible concerning the last generation.

The magnitude of transgression is measured by the corresponding light of repentance given by the saints and powered by the grace that abounds; otherwise, "sin is not imputed when there is no law" (Rom. 5:13). In short, it could be said that the full cup of iniquity is about reaching a foreknown time rather than a deadline.

> Earth's Cup of Iniquity Soon Full.—The point is fast being reached when the iniquity of transgressors will be to the full. God gives nations a certain time of probation. *He sends light and evidence, that, if received, will save them*, but if refused as the Jews refused light, indignation and punishment will fall upon them. If men refuse to be benefited, and choose darkness rather than light, they will reap the results of their choice. (Undated MS 145). (White, *The SDA Bible Commentary*, vol. 4, p. 1143, emphasis added)

Attitude of Imminent Expectation

What about imminent expectation today? We may have reached the point when this is viewed as either naïve or wishful thinking, which is understandable. Between four and six generations of the devoted have joined the sleeping saints. During their lives, they had strong evidences for hoping to see Christ's coming in their lifetime based on what appeared to be the midnight of final prophecies. Church members are nearly unanimous in their desire to see Christ return, but to claim this as a promise for our day seems missing from the conversation.

On the contrary, at the time of the end, He would rather expedite the end and not reserve a single unnecessary moment. "I came to send fire on the earth, and how I wish it were already kindled" (Luke 12:49, NKJV)! Where has imminent expectation gone? It seems to be generally fading from this generation, just when it might be embraced as one of our most cherished promises. "Watch ye therefore: for ye know not when the master of the house cometh, at even, or at midnight, or at the cockcrowing, or in the morning" (Mark 13:35).

Heaven in Our Lifetime?

This section's title should not be misunderstood as a break in Christ's instruction against predicting a date or even a timeframe for the end. Rather, it's about the potential for the present generation of saints (or any later generation, in case this one passes on the torch) to become movers of the coming of Christ. First of all, is there specific instruction from the Bible with respect to moving forward the time of His return?

Is There a Calling for His People to Shorten the Time?

Speaking to God's people (see 2 Peter 3:1, 8), Peter asks in verses 11 and 12, "Therefore, since all these things will be dissolved, what manner *of persons* ought you to be in holy conduct and godliness, looking for and hastening the coming of the day of God, because of which the heavens will be dissolved, being on fire, and the elements will melt with fervent heat" (NKJV)? This familiar text does appear to urge a shortening of the time, but to whom mainly is this verse addressed? He identifies the timeframe within the passage. "Knowing this first, that there shall come *in the last days* scoffers, walking after their own lusts, And saying, Where is the promise of his coming? for since the fathers fell asleep, all things continue as they were from the beginning of the creation. For this they willingly are ignorant of, that by the word of God the heavens were of old, and the earth standing out of the water and in the water" (vs. 3–5, emphasis added).

Corresponding to the last days, this passage suggests a period of history when "higher criticism" and godless science would deny God as the source of creation and the global flood. This proliferated from the 1700s and was joined by the theory of evolution in 1859. These were, to a large degree, successful satanic strategies to overthrow the biblical record in anticipation of the Second Advent awakening of the mid-1800s.

Another evidence that a hastening emphasis is only applicable to the last days is that Paul gives quite the opposite message to the early Christians. In 2 Thessalonians 2:1–3, he writes, "we ask you not to be soon shaken in mind or troubled, either by spirit or by word or by letter, as if from us, as though the day of Christ had come. Let no one deceive you by any means; *for that Day will not come* unless the falling away comes first, and the man of sin is revealed, the son of perdition" (NKJV, emphasis added). In contrast with Peter's call to hasten, the apostle Paul is actually cautioning against imminent expectation because hastening could not apply before the "falling away comes first, and the man of sin is revealed," which was not fulfilled until several centuries later when the Antichrist was correctly identified.

The "last days" of James 5 also identifies with our hastening era:

> "Go to now, ye rich men, weep and howl for your miseries that shall come upon you. Your riches are corrupted, and your

garments are motheaten. Your gold and silver is cankered; and the rust of them shall be a witness against you, and shall eat your flesh as it were fire. Ye have heaped treasure together for the *last days*. Behold, the hire of the labourers who have reaped down your fields, which is of you kept back by fraud, crieth: and the cries of them which have reaped are entered into the ears of the Lord of sabaoth. Ye have lived in pleasure on the earth, and been wanton; ye have nourished your hearts, as in a day of slaughter." (James 5:1–5, emphasis added)

There is nothing new about accumulating vast fortunes on the backs of cheap labor. The difference here, which James points out as being specific to our day, is a time when sudden and whole-scale economic collapse can erase the value of great wealth, as seen in a small measure by the Great Depression and major recessions. This threat only became possible with the expansion of stock trading within the last two centuries. Only recently has the entire, global, financial security been tied to international exchanges, and the economies of the nations are now all intertwined.

Verse 8 then drives home a similar emphasis to that of 2 Peter: "Be ye also patient; stablish your hearts: for the coming of the Lord draweth nigh." Another passage that speaks in particular to our time is Hebrews 10, as evidenced by verse 25, indicating a message addressed to those living in a hastening generation.

10:19—"have boldness to enter the sanctuary" (Holman Christian Standard Bible; Which apartment of the sanctuary depended on which age? Pre-1844—Holy Place; post-1844—Most Holy Place)

10:22—"with a true heart in full of assurance of faith"—for hearts sprinkled or washed from a sin-stained conscience (righteousness by faith)

10:23—holding to "the profession of our faith without wavering"

10:24—love one another

10:25—"Not forsaking the assembly of ourselves...*as ye see the day approaching*" (the context here applies this chapter mainly to those living near the end)

10:26, 27—In the final days when the end is imminent, if believers "sin willfully after" receiving "the knowledge of truth, there remaineth no more sacrifice," but judgment

10:28–30—"...The Lord shall judge His people" (a judgment future to Paul's day)

10:32, 33—"call to remembrance the former days...whilst ye were made a gazingstock both by reproaches and afflictions" (true for the early Christians as well as the last Christians)

10:34—a time of ruining our earthly goods in favor of what awaits us above

10:35, 36—"Cast not away therefore your confidence...ye have need of patience, *that, after ye have done will of God* [roles of the saints are satisfied], *ye might receive the promise*" (and the promise is...)

10:37—This verse then quotes Habakkuk 2:3: "For yet a little while, and he that shall come will come, and will not tarry" (not delay any further since the saints have done the will of God)

This is an early glimpse on how to grasp His appearing within our lifetime as a promise.

In Habakkuk 2, the words previous to those quoted above state the manner by which the saints approach God for unlimited grace. They place themselves where they may obtain the best view and hearing of the Spirit of God (more on this shortly). "I will stand upon my watch, and set me upon the tower, and will watch to see what he will say unto me, and what I shall answer when I am reproved. And the LORD answered me, and said, Write the vision, and make it plain upon tables, that he may run that readeth it. *For the vision is yet for an appointed time, but at the end it shall speak, and not lie: though it tarry, wait for it; because it will surely come, it will not tarry"* (1–3, emphasis added).

Another "hasten" verse is Isaiah 60:22: "I the LORD will hasten it in his time." This chapter, in symbolic language, describes a future in connection with the harvest of the saved from the nations. The first verses indicate a partnership of God and His people by which He hastens it. "Arise, shine; for thy light has come…"

Every good work is by His Spirit and grace from above, but if His people's role can be narrowed down to something that is solely their own doing, it is simply the response of choosing to have perfect faith in Him. "Now the just shall live by faith…" (Heb. 10:38).

The Power to Delay or Expedite

Delay, rather than the will of God, persists only until mercy is exhausted, yet hastening will prevail over delay when all the required pieces of the divine plan are in place. Returning to 2 Peter 3, we have both opposing principles: the quickening of the day of God as seen in verse 12 above, and the delaying as found here in verse 9: "The Lord is not slack concerning his promise, as some men count slackness; but is longsuffering to us-ward, not willing that any should perish, but that all should come to repentance."

The delay word in this verse is "slackness." The cause of the delay is those to whom the Lord is extending mercy, and so as Peter records, it is not the Lord who is slacking, but His children ("us-ward") who delay in coming to full repentance. The implication is clear: repentance of people through faith helps shorten the delay. Could a revival of repentance and return to righteous living by faith reduce further delay and permit quickening instead? Peter confirms this in Acts 3:19–20: "Repent ye therefore, and be converted, that your sins may be blotted out, *when* the times of refreshing shall come from the presence of the Lord. *And he shall send Jesus Christ*, which before was preached unto you" (emphasis added).

"Clearly this idea of hastening the End is the corollary of the explanation [2 Peter 3:9] that God defers the Parousia because he desires Christians to repent. Their repentance and holy living may therefore, from the human standpoint, hasten its coming. This does not detract from God's sovereignty in determining the time of the End ... but means only that his sovereign determination graciously takes human affairs into account" (Bauckham, *Jude–2 Peter, Volume 50,* p. 325).

The sense of 2 Peter 3:9 is that when it is time to hasten, Jesus is delaying, but not arbitrarily. If only one person has been putting off repentance and therefore, salvation, then the Lord will hold off His coming if, by His infinite knowledge, He sees that a little more time will alter eternity for that person. At this time, delay, although merciful, is really further disappointment when considering what continues with each passing day—new depths of violence, war, pestilence, corruption, natural disasters, etc.

> The third watch calls for threefold earnestness. To become impatient now would to lose all our earnest, persevering watching heretofore. The long night of gloom is trying; but the morning is deferred in mercy, because if the Master should come, so many would be found unready. God's unwillingness to have his people perish has been the reason of so long delay. But the coming of the morning to the faithful, and of the night to the unfaithful, is right upon us. By waiting and watching, God's people are to manifest their peculiar character, their separation from the world. By our watching positions we are to show that we are truly strangers and pilgrims upon the earth. (White, *Testimonies for the Church*, vol. 2, p. 194)

By giving the gospel to the world it is in our power to hasten our Lord's return. We are not only to look for but to hasten the coming of the day of God. 2 Peter 3:12, margin. Had the church of Christ done her appointed work as the Lord ordained, the whole world would before this have been warned, and the Lord Jesus would have come to our earth in power and great glory. (White, *The Desire of Ages*, p. 633)

We have long been looking and waiting for the coming of the Lord; but are we doing all in our power to hasten his coming? "The Lord is not slack concerning his promise, as some men count slackness; but is longsuffering to usward, not willing that any should perish, but that all should come to repentance." While the Lord is *ever* working, while all heaven is engaged in the work on earth to *draw men to Christ and repentance*, what are the human agents doing to be channels of light, that they may co-operate with the divine agencies? Are they daily inquiring, "Lord, what wilt thou have me to do?" Are they practicing self-denial, as did Jesus? Are they deeply stirred, their hearts drawn out in prayer to God that they may be receiving of his grace, the Holy Spirit of God, that they may have wisdom to work with their ability and their means to save souls that are perishing out of Christ? (White, *The Review and Herald*, May 16, 1893 par. 12, emphasis added)

Only in mercy has He made allowance for delay, and not for any other reason, because the time given for human misery was never meant to linger during the last moments of history. In what manner does God address spiritual stagnation in the last days? Jesus and history show that great light, if not heeded, leads to a proportional darkness. Thus, God's response to break this trend is to reluctantly intervene by using a great crisis, along with a hope message of such a nature as to arouse His people from delay mode to acceleration. Would not the need for crises thus diminish due to a renewed dedication to hasting the end since opportunity is knocking? There are weeks and days dedicated to revival and reformation. What if special days of the calendar were set aside for confession, repentance, and revival, especially when considering the power that repentance has for reducing delay?

Hastening Objections

A biblical parallel over the hasten/delay potential comes from the last scene in Numbers 13. After the heads of the twelve tribes of Israel returned from spying out the Promised Land, ten of the twelve expressed complaints based upon a reliance on the demographical statistics of their day. Only two had faith in God despite appearances. The plan was that after the spies returned, the whole congregation would gain immediate entrance to their promised homeland. Instead, as the record shows, through unbelief, there was not another opportunity for forty years. If Joshua and Caleb were living today, their testimony would be nearly the same.

"And Caleb stilled the people…and said, *Let us go up at once*, and possess it; for we are well able to overcome it" (v. 30, emphasis added). Yes, today we are called to claim, with full assurance, the promise of Christ's return "at once" (in our lifetime).

Is the interpretation of "hasten" only about speeding up the time? What are the objections? Not many, but there are a couple to consider.

1. As for a common objection, if we try to hasten Christ, wouldn't that result in far fewer people who are ready?

    Although the Lord made it clear that few find the narrow way (see Matt. 7:14), how do we define "few"? It depends on the greater number with which "few" is compared. For the seven to eight billion now living on earth, few would be multiple millions. It should be no surprise that our Friend has the solution for this concern well in advance. Is it possible for His disciples today to both quicken the end through His aid and also realize the innumerable harvest of living saints that God seeks? As we shall find, the two outcomes do coincide.

2. What is the certainty that the word "hasting" (2 Peter 3:12) can only be interpreted as hurrying Christ's return?

    On the meaning of "hasting," one objection is in the form of an alternative interpretation. It is said that the use of "hasting" by Peter is thought to have been used only in passing, referring to the people's attention being riveted on the primary event of the passage as they see it coming, "Since all these things [elements of the earth] are to be destroyed…" followed by a "new heavens and a new earth…" (vs. 11, 13, NASB).

There are Greek interlinear Bibles that take up this variant meaning and translate "hasting" as "eagerly" so that the text would say, "looking for and awaiting eagerly the coming of the day of God."

"This is a striking suggestion, that men, in some way, can speed up God's plans" (Payne, 1969, p. 604). "Such an understanding does not commend itself to all commentators; but there is no good reason for rejecting it. Peter implied the same thing. No! He said the same thing in Acts 3:19–21" (StudyLight, http://1ref.us/nw [accessed 08/16/2018]).

How is 2 Peter 3:12 translated in some English versions? The KJV, Tyndale, Geneva, and others say we are "Looking for and *hasting unto* the coming of the day of God," implying an immovable and fixed day, and it is we on earth who, in our short lives, are hastening ourselves to the coming of the Lord. However, the NKJV and NASB leave out the word "unto" and read, "looking for and hastening the coming of the day of God." The NIV says "as you look forward to the day of God and speed its coming." These last versions rather conclusively portray the meaning as "speed" or "accelerate" the coming of the day of God.

The Greek word for "hasting" in 2 Peter 3:12 is "speudo" (4692 in *Strong's*). "Speudo" is a root word—one that is a simple building block for other words. It is not derived from any other words. It turns out that "speudo" has a one-word English translation—"speed"—which has nearly the same spelling and pronunciation.

In modern English, "speed" can refer to rate of travel, swiftness, speed reading; there is not much variation of meaning. The same is true of four of the five New Testament passages in which the word "speudo" is found. In the first four, a faster pace of movement is clearly indicated. As for 2 Peter 3:12, the idea of quickening the time may not appear as obvious but there is really nothing in the text to suggest otherwise.

"And they came with haste [*speudo*], and found Mary, and Joseph, and the babe lying in a manger" (Luke 2:16). The shepherds, filled with amazement from the sight of rejoicing angels filling the night sky, had no thought of sticking around with their flocks. The headed off immediately with a sense of urgency to relate what they had just experienced.

"And when Jesus came to the place, he looked up [into a tree], and saw him, and said unto him, Zacchaeus, make haste [*speudo*], and come down; for to day I must abide at thy house. And he [Zacchaeus] made haste [*speudo*], and came down, and received him [Jesus] joyfully" (Luke 19:5, 6). What Zaccheus heard was not a request to take his time getting down from the tree but to come down in a hurry—another way of saying "I can't wait to visit you at your house."

"For Paul had determined to sail by Ephesus, because he would not spend the time in Asia: for he hasted [*speudo*], if it were possible for him, to be at Jerusalem the day of Pentecost" (Acts 20:16). Paul knew that travel often comes with unplanned delays, so speed was of utmost importance in order to make Pentecost on time. That meant no stopping in Asia overnight.

"And saw him saying unto me, Make haste [*speudo*], and get thee quickly out of Jerusalem: for they will not receive thy testimony concerning me" (Acts 22:18). Evidently, labor in Jerusalem had begun to be a misuse of time, thus the call to hurriedly begin gospel labor for the Gentiles.

"Looking for and hasting [*speudo*] unto the coming of the day of God, wherein the heavens being on fire shall be dissolved, and the elements shall melt with fervent heat" (2 Peter 3:12). As noted above, in this King James verse, the word "unto" is supplied by the King James Bible translators.

This leaves "speudo" standing alone, which thankfully shows the value of the other passages using "speudo" in giving this word its proper meaning: "speed the day of God."

Although *speudo* equates with "speed," Peter's more precise thought was more in line with "acceleration," which is continually increasing speed, rather than a one-time increase. From physics, velocity (speed) is constant movement at a *steady pace*. Acceleration is increasingly greater velocity relative to time. Arrival time is guaranteed to be sooner if a vehicle even once accelerates during the trip. Indeed, the end is speeding toward us and always has been since our planet first fell into the curse of death, but the call to hasten—at the right time—is really a call to accelerate.

If we are now living during the time capsule of 2 Peter 3:12 when the emphasis is on acceleration, then what explains why anyone would settle with the mindset that we have nothing to do about the timing? 'He will come when He is ready' is the thought of many. However, let's step back and look at the idea of earnestly awaiting. Yes, this principle is found in 2 Peter 3:12, but rather than "hasting," the earnest awaiting is represented by the preceding phrase, "Looking for." Yes, today it is as important to eagerly look for the Lord as it is to hasten Him!

The Instrumental Closing Events Depend on Inside Signs Rather Than Outward Ones

Destroying events, such as those described by Jesus in Matthew 24 and in the seven trumpets in Revelation 8 and 9, may have stirred Christians to revival mindedness, but of themselves, these judgments are not signs of Christ's coming, but warnings to seek the help of God for preparing to meet Him.

Today, as in the past, it is popular to tie the second coming only to dramatic outer signs, wonders, and disasters. Yet nothing has more impact on the second coming than what is accomplished in His church, and this is really the next turning point.

As keenly as people now ponder the concept of the end, the disciples also did. Before departing from earth, Jesus made a clarification of what the disciples had misunderstood. When they asked, "Tell us, when shall these things be? and what shall be the sign of thy coming, and of the end of the world" (Matt. 24:3), their question reflected the belief that the last day depended on signs rather than on themselves. Although Jesus did answer with far-reaching outward signs, they mostly served to caution the early and latter disciples about what was to personally affect them. Then again, the key end-determining event would come from His people. He emphasized the sign of those who endure to the end, whose love does not wax cold, and enduring love is the overall character that will permit the preaching of the gospel to be carried to all nations (see vs. 12–14).

"Our world is a vast lazar house, a scene of misery that we dare not allow even our thoughts to dwell upon. Did we realize it as it is, the burden would be too terrible. Yet God feels it all. In order to destroy sin and its results He gave His best Beloved, and He has put it in our power, through co-operation with Him, to bring this scene of misery to an end" (White 1903, p. 264). How priceless then must His last-day witnesses appear to the heavenly hosts, given the potential they have through grace for affecting the destiny of an entire generation.

Chapter 2

Holy Festivals Foretell and Typify the Restoration Journey

Preparing the Way

Delighted as God is to have Enoch, Elijah, Moses, and others with Him now, our Creator is a God of myriads. Consider the numbers of angels accompanying our Savior as recorded in Daniel 7:10 and Revelation 5:11—thousands of thousands and ten thousand times ten thousand. When we imagine from where these angels probably are—other worlds that orbit sun-like stars, of which there are now estimated to be millions of trillions in the universe—then God certainly misses having a myriad of us. If it were possible for fallen humanity, limited in our physical and fallen state, to endure the direct presence of God, He might well have been appearing to mankind all along. However, when we regain our supernatural makeup at the resurrection, in addition to dwelling comfortably in His glory, we will also have nearly unlimited capacities, such as a travel time to the Orion Nebula, reduced from 1,600 light years to merely several earth days. "We all entered the cloud together, and were seven days ascending to the sea of glass" (White, *Early Writings*, p. 16).

Until that translation day, the Lord gives us a sanctuary, a space where mortals can meet with the eternal One. "And let them make me a sanctuary; that I may dwell among them" (Exod. 25:8). Through Christ's sanctuary movements as High Priest, He is working out both a decisive end of fallen earth and a multitude to meet Him in the clouds.

Although the cross brought an end to the Old Testament ceremonies and rituals tied to the earthly sanctuary, there is much symbolism representing Jesus Christ and our redemption through His sacrifice. For us today, the sanctuary is a place accessible through prayer, with only a veil or curtain between us and God in His temple above. Hebrews 10:20 says that veil is the humanity of the Son of God.

> *Through Christ's sanctuary movements as High Priest, He is working out both a decisive end of fallen earth and a multitude to meet Him in the clouds.*

As hinted in the book of Colossians, special sanctuary times serve prophetically as shadows of things to come. The annual holidays, in particular, concern the succession of Christ's restoration activities over the entire Christian era, starting from the last supper with His disciples and ending with His return (see Heb. 9:1–12; 10:1). Prophetic fulfillment of each feast type represents a milestone on the road of completing God's plan of salvation.

"Let no man therefore judge you in meat, or in drink, or in respect of an holyday, or of the new moon, or of the sabbath days: 17 Which are a shadow of things to come; but the body is of Christ" (Col. 2:16, 17). In other words, let no one bother you about participating in the ceremonies which now only find meaning in their symbolic representations, centered in Christ Jesus (To clarify, the Sabbath rest, as required in the ten-commandment moral law, is distinguished from the Levitical sacrifices of that day. Colossians 2:16 only refers to ceremonial law. Verse 17 brings to light their prophetic significance. See also Hebrews 10:1.).

The table below gives an idea of interactivity between God and His people that characterizes a completed restoration. Though the saints have their roles, even these are fully dependent on His grace working in them. "Every good gift and every perfect gift is from above, and cometh down from the Father of lights" (James 1:17). The first and second church tasks give rise to a people who prepare the way of the Lord, as did Elijah and John the Baptist in their times.

	Annual Feast Type	Outcome
1.	**Passover:** Sacrifice of the Lamb of God (1 Cor. 5:7) and **First Fruits** (1 Cor. 15:20)	Foundation of all other fulfillments, the death and resurrection of Jesus Christ
2.	**Pentecost: Early Rain** of the gospel commission (Matt. 28:19) and the **Small Rains** for growing the crops	First release of Divine power, then **First Church task:** recover from the Dark Ages through the Reformation, laying the ground for the end-time remnant.
3.	**Day of Trumpets:** Sound of alarm through crises—the Day of Judgment approaches.	Christ our High Priest in review of the books during the hour of judgment, then **Second Church task:** the remnant fully reflecting Christ's character
4.	**Day of Atonement/Pre-Advent judgment:** everlasting (finishing) gospel	
5.	**Day of Tabernacles** (Booths): **Latter Rain** ("second Pentecost"), **Sealing**, and **Return of Christ** for harvest Reaping (Zech. 14)	Final release of divine power, then **Third and Fourth Remnant Church tasks:** finishing the gospel and filling God's house

First of all, upon what indispensable roles are God's people to unite, which help produce a triumphant return of Christ? The following are selections from Ellen G. White's inspired commentary, which lay out their hastening tasks (Her writings are cited frequently in this document. They are considered to be counsel and inspired Bible commentary in fulfillment of the provisions promised to the church in Romans 12:6–8, 1 Corinthians 12:4–10, and Ephesians 4:8–11).

Rise of the Reformation out of which Emerges the Advent Movement

Like the great Reformation of the sixteenth century, the advent movement appeared in different countries of Christendom at the same time. In both Europe and America men of faith and prayer were led to the study of the prophecies, and, tracing down the inspired record, they saw convincing evidence that the end of all things was at hand. In different lands there were isolated bodies of Christians who, solely by the study of the Scriptures, arrived at the belief that the Saviour's advent was near. (White, *The Great* Controversy, p. 357)

Looking down through the ages to the close of time, Peter was inspired to outline conditions that would exist in the world just prior to the second coming of Christ. "There shall come in the last days scoffers," he wrote, "walking after their own lusts, and saying, Where is the promise of His coming? for since the fathers fell asleep, all things continue as they were from the beginning of the creation." But "when they shall say, Peace and safety; then sudden destruction cometh upon them." 1 Thessalonians 5:3. Not all, however, would be ensnared by the enemy's devices. As the end of all things earthly should approach, there would be faithful ones able to discern the signs of the times. While a large number of professing believers would deny their faith by their works, there would be <u>a remnant who would endure to the end</u>. (White, *Acts of the Apostles*, pp. 535–536, emphasis added)

Remnant Reflecting the Character of Christ

Christ is waiting with longing desire for the manifestation of Himself in His church. When the character of the Saviour shall be perfectly reproduced in His people, then He will come to claim His own. It is the privilege of every Christian, not only to look for, but to hasten, the coming of our Lord. (White, *Maranatha*, p. 112)

A reliable indicator of divine character is the beneficent use of our personal resources.

God Himself originates the plans for the advancement of His work, and He has provided His people with a surplus of means, that when He calls for help, they may cheerfully respond. If they will be faithful in bringing to His treasury the means lent them, His work will make rapid advancement. Many souls will be won to the truth, and the day of Christ's coming will be hastened.— *R. & H., July 14, 1904*. (White, *Counsels on Stewardship*, p. 45)

Give the light to others by giving of your means to send workers into new fields. Thus you will hasten the coming of Christ. He who is truly converted will feel it a privilege to give of his means to send the truth into the dark places of the earth. (White, *The Review and Herald*, February 4, 1904, par. 5)

If those to whom God's money has been entrusted will be faithful in bringing the means lent them to the Lord's treasury, His work will make rapid advancement. Many souls will be won to the cause of truth, and the day of Christ's coming will be hastened. (White, *Testimonies for the Church*, vol. 9, p. 58)

Proclaim the Gospel Until It Covers the Globe

Christ sent forth His disciples with the message, "The kingdom of God is at hand." The proclamation of this message is our work. Jesus said, "This Gospel of the kingdom shall be preached in all the world for a witness unto all nations." His kingdom will not come until the good tidings of His grace have been carried to all the earth. Let us proclaim the message, "Behold the Lamb of God, which taketh away the sin of the world." Thus we may hasten the coming of the Saviour. (White, *The Signs of the Times*, October 28, 1903, par. 6)

Hence, as we give ourselves to God, and win other souls to Him, we hasten the coming of His kingdom. Only those who devote themselves to His service, saying, "Here am I; send me" (Isaiah 6:8), to open blind eyes, to turn men "from darkness to light and from the power of Satan unto God, that they may receive forgiveness of sins and inheritance among them which are sanctified" (Acts 26:18)—they alone pray in sincerity, "Thy kingdom come." (White, *Thoughts from the Mount of Blessing*, p. 109)

Were all who profess His name bearing fruit to His glory, how quickly the whole world would be sown with the seed of the

> gospel. Quickly the last harvest would be ripened, and Christ would come to gather the precious grain.
>
> My brethren and sisters, plead for the Holy Spirit, God stands back of every promise He has made. With your Bibles in your hands, say: "I have done as Thou hast said, I present Thy promise, 'Ask, and it shall be given you; seek, and ye shall find; knock, and it shall be opened unto you.'" (White, *Testimonies for the Church*, vol. 8, p. 22–23)

Since the annual holidays are tied to harvest thanksgiving, they provide a framework for this section, following the "food chain" of an agrarian community beginning with heaven's timely watering of the earth after seed-sowing. Then ripening rains assure fruitful yearly harvests and thus strength and health for the future.

1. Seed Planting
2. Early Sprouting Rain and Growth Rain
3. Weeding or Pruning
4. Crop Inspection
5. Ripening Rain

Each level of maturity provides direction for preparing the guests of the bride, New Jerusalem, for the wedding with Christ and, allegorically, as crops for the second coming harvest. "And he said, So is the kingdom of God, as if a man should cast seed into the ground; And should sleep, and rise night and day, and the seed should spring and grow up, he knoweth not how. For the earth bringeth forth fruit of herself; first the blade, then the ear, after that the full corn in the ear. But when the fruit is brought forth, *immediately* he putteth in the sickle, because the harvest is come" (Mark 4:26–29, emphasis added). Therefore, whatever it takes to grow this fruit to harvest ripening is an activity of the highest order today, in heaven and on earth.

Passover and First Fruits

"These are the feasts of the LORD, even holy convocations, which ye shall proclaim in their seasons. In the fourteenth day of the first month at even is the LORD's passover. And on the fifteenth day of the same month is the feast of unleavened bread unto the LORD: seven days ye must eat unleavened bread" (Lev. 23:4–6).

"Purge out therefore the old leaven, that ye may be a new lump, as ye are unleavened. For even Christ our passover is sacrificed for us" (1 Cor. 5:7).

"And he said unto them, With desire I have desired to eat this passover with you before I suffer: For I say unto you, I will not any more eat thereof, until it be fulfilled in the kingdom of God. And he took the cup, and gave thanks, and said, Take this, and divide it among yourselves: For I say unto you, I will not drink of the fruit of the vine, until the kingdom of God shall come" (Luke 22:15–18).

The loftiest theme of Scripture is that all the fruits of salvation ever produced find their origin at the cross and resurrection of Christ.

The loftiest theme of Scripture is that all the fruits of salvation ever produced find their origin at the cross and resurrection of Christ.

> And he said unto them, These are the words which I spake unto you, while I was yet with you, that all things must be fulfilled, which were written in the law of Moses, and in the prophets, and in the psalms, concerning Me. Then opened he their understanding, that they might understand the scriptures, And said unto them, Thus it is written, and thus it behooved Christ to suffer, and to rise from the dead the third day: And that repentance and remission of sins should be preached in his name among all nations, beginning at Jerusalem. And ye are witnesses of these things." (Luke 24:44–48)

"And Jesus answered them, saying, The hour is come, that the Son of man should be glorified. Verily, verily, I say unto you, Except a corn of wheat fall into the ground and die, it abideth alone: but if it die, it bringeth forth much fruit" (John 12:23).

"Speak unto the children of Israel, and say unto them, When ye be come into the land which I give unto you, and shall reap the harvest thereof, then ye shall bring a sheaf of the firstfruits of your harvest unto the priest: And he shall wave the sheaf before the LORD, to be accepted for you: on the morrow after the sabbath the priest shall wave it" (Lev. 23:10, 11).

"But now is Christ risen from the dead, and become the firstfruits of them that slept" (1 Cor. 15:20).

Pentecost Shadow Fulfillment and the First of Three Bible Rains

Annual Feast Type	Outcome
2. **Pentecost: Early Rain** of the Gospel commission (Mat. 28:19) and the **Small Rains** for growing the crops	First release of Divine power, then 1st Church task—recover from the Dark Ages through the Reformation, laying the ground for the end-time Remnant.

"And ye shall count unto you from the morrow after the sabbath, from the day that ye brought the sheaf of the wave offering; seven sabbaths shall be complete: Even unto the morrow after the seventh sabbath shall ye number fifty days; and ye shall offer a new meat offering unto the LORD" (Lev. 23:15, 16). This was Pentecost, which means "fiftieth."

For an introduction of the symbolic rains, the literal counterparts are the seasonal Palestinian rains. By the blessing of God, the rains came at their appointed times, making possible the corresponding, annual, Jewish holidays.

"Be glad then, ye children of Zion, and rejoice in the LORD your God: for he hath given you the former rain moderately, and he will cause to come down for you the rain, the former rain, and the latter rain in the first month. And the floors shall be full of wheat, and the vats shall overflow with wine and oil" (Joel 2:23, 24). This passage represents a dual fulfillment, symbolized by the seasonal rains of Palestine.

The three seasons of moisture are timed for germination, growing, and harvest ripening. Each harvest began with a thanksgiving commemoration to God for His rains: Pentecost, with a lesser harvest in the spring, and Tabernacles in the fall, combining both the early and latter rain for the abundant harvest before "the great and awesome day of the Lord" (v. 31, NKJV).

Early Rain

Souls, like seed, have life in them, ready to spring out of the ground through the early rain. Although this rain sprouted the early church 2,000 years ago, it is included as a "final movement" because it still provides a continued role today. Historically, the first outpouring was God's startup power, giving the church a grounded presence on earth: "…the early rain fell upon the disciples on the Day of Pentecost" (White 1889, p. 214).

After that time of New Testament activation described in Acts 1, the early rain refreshing has been imparted where gospel preaching has been conducted—among a locality where previously it was forgotten or never heard. It is the gospel groundbreaking, indwelling, and manifestation of the Holy Spirit to previously unreached souls and those who have returned to Him.

The first outpouring of the Holy Spirit continues to be instrumental until the end, given for the life-transforming conversion of every believer. Although, since that first Pentecost, the outward wonders of this visitation of divine power have greatly diminished, they will return during the last visitation before the return of Christ.

What exactly are the "times of refreshing"? Does this expression from Acts 3:19 directly correspond to the rain of the Holy Spirit? Also, is a simple thing like repentance the most immediate key condition for the rain to be outpoured? According to Acts 2:38–39, the answer is yes to both questions. While the early rain was in progress, "Peter said unto them, Repent, and be baptized every one of you in the name of Jesus Christ for the remission of sins, and ye shall receive the gift of the Holy Ghost. For the promise is unto you, and to your children, and to all that are afar off, even as many as the Lord our God shall call."

Dew and Small Rains

What about life over the long haul for the Christian, the church, and the world between the two outpourings? The Bible and Spirit of Prophecy also mention the morning growing dews and small rains (seasons of growing revivals). "Give ear, O ye heavens, and I will speak; and hear, O earth, the words of my mouth. My doctrine shall drop as the rain, my speech shall distil as the dew, as the small rain upon the tender herb, and as the showers upon the grass" (Deut. 32:1, 2). When His teaching shall drop as the rain, its moisture comes to refresh every soul standing under its showers. "Divine grace is needed at the beginning, divine grace at every step of advance, and divine grace alone can complete the work" (White 1923, p. 508).

There is spiritual moisture between the early and latter rains for growing the seedlings to maturity when they are ready for fruiting. This moisture comes mostly in the mornings, as does the dew or small rains that may seem to be just enough to keep the sprouts growing. It is a time of testing when each plant is helped to endure as much as grow. The dew is not the beginning or finishing rain, but the growing rain. "I will be as the dew unto Israel: he shall grow as the lily, and cast forth his roots as Lebanon" (Hosea 14:5).

The plant, the child, grows by receiving from its surroundings that which ministers to its life—air, sunshine, and food. What these gifts of nature are to animal and plant, such is Christ to those who trust in Him. He is their "everlasting light," "a sun and shield." Isaiah 60:19; Psalm 84:11. He shall be as "the dew unto Israel." "He shall come down like rain upon the mown grass." Hosea 14:5; Psalm 72:6. He is the living water, "the Bread of God ... which cometh down from heaven, and giveth life unto the world." John 6:33. (White, *Steps to Christ*, p. 68)

Dew appeared early in the morning, and in its place was found manna. "And when the dew that lay was gone up, behold, upon the face of the wilderness there lay a small round thing, as small as the hoar frost on the ground. And when the children of Israel saw it, they said one to another, It is manna: for they wist not what it was. And Moses said unto them, This is the bread which the LORD hath given you to eat" (Exod. 16:14, 15). For us today, manna is the bread and grace of His Word gathered up morning by morning.

With these initial and continuing rains, the first hastening task of believers was to give rise to the Reformation to counter the falling away of the church during the early centuries. During the Dark Ages, the early rain was nearly extinguished as a result of the established church uniting with paganistic rites and man-made traditions. Then the rain rebounded during the start of the Protestant Reformation.

The eventual jewel of the Reformation would be the uniting of a people who give earth's final message at the key time of history, when the last time prophecy ended in 1844. Long story short, through the lessons of faith gained from the Reformation and its trials, the opening up of end-time prophecies, and the grace of God, they endure to the end. Revelation 12 through 14 refers to these believers collectively as the remnant. For the most part, they obtain the Lord's shelter against being swept up by the dragon's deceiving arts and authority over society. True to the inspired record, they sprang up from the Millerite revival of the early 1800s, culminating on October 22, 1844, the day which fulfilled the bittersweet experience of Revelation 10.

During the final release of God's power, they prophesy again (see v. 11) and continue until Jesus returns (14:12–14). They correspond to the last Elijah that Jesus and Old Testament prophecy foretold will come, restoring God's original design (see Matt. 17:11).

Latter Rain

The latter rain is reviewed here, but in the setting of Advent hastening during the last outpouring is expanded under the Feast of Tabernacles, chapter 4.

Though, regretfully, the spiritual power of first-century Pentecost has greatly diminished, it will return with the latter rain, even exceeding the former. In God's wisdom, however, the Spirit may not operate in quite the same manner. Joel expressed the extent of the spiritual gifts given:

> And it shall come to pass afterward, that I will pour out My spirit upon all flesh; your sons and your daughters shall prophesy, your old men shall dream dreams, your young men shall see visions: And also upon the servants and upon the handmaids in those days will I pour out my spirit. And I will shew wonders in the heavens and in the earth, blood, and fire, and pillars of smoke. The sun shall be turned into darkness, and the moon into blood, before the great and the terrible day of the LORD come. And it shall come to pass, that whosoever shall call on the name of the LORD shall be delivered: for in mount Zion and in Jerusalem shall be deliverance, as the LORD hath said, and in the remnant whom the LORD shall call. (Joel 2:28–32)

In Joel 2 is found a scriptural anchor concerning the intent of the first task (the end-time rise of the remnant), along with the second task ("sanctify the congregation," v. 16), leading to the last outpouring ("the latter rain," v. 23). "It is left with us to remedy the defects in our characters, to cleanse the soul temple of every defilement. Then the latter rain will fall upon us as the early rain fell upon the disciples on the Day of Pentecost" (White 1889, p. 214). It is then that the third task will be accomplished. "And this gospel of the kingdom shall be preached in all the world for a witness unto all nations; and then shall the end come" (Matt. 24:14). This is tied to Revelation 14:6–12.

The calling, from the early church and through the centuries until the arrival of the remnant, has been the gospel, but near the end, it elevates to the everlasting gospel, being salvaged from ages of distortion by superstition, ceremony, and formality. The everlasting component of the gospel represents its ultimate clarity of understanding and simplicity, so that it would qualify as the final call of salvation. This results from the growing dews and small rains.

The latter rain is the grace that makes their efforts amplify, comparable to the thousands fed by a few loaves and fishes. At that time, unprecedented success will be seen, compared to past labors.

> Gather the people, sanctify the congregation…Let the priests, who minister to the LORD, Weep between the porch and the altar; Let them say, "Spare Your people, O LORD, And do not give Your heritage to reproach, That the nations should rule over them. Why should they say among the peoples, 'Where *is* their God?'" Then the LORD will be zealous for His land, And pity His people. The LORD will answer and say to His people, "Behold, I will send you grain and new wine and oil, And you will be satisfied by them; I will no longer make you a reproach among the nations." (Joel 2:16–19, NKJV)

In answer to their prayers, the grain, new wine, and oil appear. In symbol, these represent the threefold provisions for obtaining the growing level of sanctification: 1) "grain" is the gospel light of the Word (see Matt. 4:4), 2) "wine" is the centrality of the redeeming blood of Christ (see 1 Cor. 11:25), and 3) "oil" symbolizes the Holy Spirit applying the grain and wine to human vessels (see 1 Sam. 16:13; Zech. 4). Once His people have been gathered and sanctified, then the grain, wine, and oil are plentiful by the outpouring rain.

Chapter 3

Trumpets and Solemn Day of Atonement Shadow Fulfillments

Taking hastening to the next level is Christ's judgment activity as recorded in Revelation 8, 9, and 14:6–7, which started immediately after the formation of the remnant. This is the movement of heaven which transitions the earth from basically the entire 2,000 years since Christ ascended to the next brief era, when the harvest is gathered from the world for His return. Included in this event are not only the remnant, but Christians of all persuasions.

Although established as the rescue plan even before the fall of Adam and Eve (see Rev. 13:8b), this is the inward character restoration of the remnant which, when accomplished as a whole, opens the door for the last two tasks to be completed within a single generation. The following statements introduce the importance of this transformed congregation in God's plans:

"The Lord would have his church purified, before his judgments shall fall more signally upon the world" (White, *The Review and Herald*, November 8, 1906, par. 1).

"I saw that God could carry on His work without any of man's help; but this is not His plan. The present world is designed as a scene of probation for man. He is here to form a character which will pass with Him into the eternal world" (White 1868, p. 196).

Returning to the hastening text (2 Peter 3:12), the previous verse (11) sets forth this task: "Seeing then that all these things shall be dissolved, what manner of persons ought ye to be in all holy conversation and godliness…?" As a goal for His hastened coming, this is not only about personal readiness, but just as important in the larger scheme, corporate representation.

Instead of leaving us oblivious to what happens if we help Him, He provides incentive, such as attracting the remnant by promise. In the case of Christlike character by repentance through faith, He lets the remnant know that if they will enter this faith level daily, the result will be more than thinking they *might* live to see His appearing, but promises that they *will* live to see it, in particular during this time of golden opportunity we enjoy today (see Heb. 10:35–37).

Annual Feast Type	Outcome
3. **Day of Trumpets:** Sound of alarm through crises—the Day of Judgment approaches.	Christ our High Priest in review of the books during the hour of judgment, then 2nd Church task, the Remnant fully reflecting Christ's character
4. **Day of Atonement: Pre-Advent judgment**, everlasting (finishing) gospel	

The hearing of the word "judgment" commonly evokes a sense of dread, like sirens blaring when funnel clouds are bearing down. From heaven's perspective, although the trumpets have given fearful warnings, the proceeding judgment has been greatly anticipated. Thus, the saints may view it with the intensity of interest as the rising dawn (see Hosea 6:3) scatters the age-long darkness hanging over earth. Yes, the outlook of this judgment points to a supreme celebration; its effect is a bridging of the gap of long ages, ushering in the day of Christ more rapidly. By combining both warning and mercy, the trumpets and pre-advent judgment prepare for earth's closing and sealing movements. They provide a transition period so that the closing events and return of Christ are not so abrupt as to lose individuals who would otherwise be prepared through its saving activities. Uniting with the latter rain, this message proceeds with such infinite wisdom as to both save multitudes and also quicken the end.

> *By combining both warning and mercy, the trumpets and pre-advent judgment prepare for earth's closing and sealing movements.*

Yes, starting off with a warning, the judgment ends with a celebration, the very thing that a warning is not supposed to represent, but that's how the crises of the trumpets conclude—a good ending, the joining of the Bridegroom and His bride, the New Jerusalem, with the ransomed of the Lord inhabiting the mansions prepared for them.

Receiving an invitation to a wedding is the fitting symbol of the pre-advent judgment for believers seeking for the coming of Christ in their lifetime. Therefore, when Jesus is found speaking the language of this judgment, He uses the wedding theme, as seen in the three parables ahead in the second phase.

First Phase—Jesus in the Sanctuary Sends Seven Trumpeting Angels

"Speak unto the children of Israel, saying, In the seventh month, in the first day of the month, shall ye have a sabbath, a memorial of blowing of trumpets, an holy convocation" (Lev. 23:24). Given that the blowing of these 7 trumpets occurred only 9 days prior to the Day of Atonement, their purpose was clearly to alert the people of the coming holy convocation. Since solemn soul searching would be required in order to be cleansed and not "cut off" the Lord in mercy gave advance notice of the coming judgment. In their shadow fulfillment found in Revelation 8 and 9, the trumpets begin with a sad turn for the church, which began with widespread salvation power. Within the next generation, the early church already began its decline, and the trumpets sounded whenever apostasy was about to deliver its final blow. Then the church was allowed to slide into fiery trials and affliction, allowing a purifying process which led to the Reformation.

The sixth trumpet shows the extent of the church's apostasy as indicated by the severity of the trumpet's fulfillment.

> And the sixth angel sounded, and I heard a voice from the four horns of the golden altar which is before God, Saying to the sixth angel which had the trumpet, Loose the four angels which are bound in the great river Euphrates. And the four angels were loosed, which were prepared for an hour, and a day, and a month, and a year, for to slay the third part of men. (Revelation 9:13–15)

Instead of total destruction, the church came through this purifying ordeal during the sixth trumpet and historically, as well as prophetically, the remnant movement formed out of the dust.

> And such as do wickedly against the covenant shall he corrupt by flatteries: but the people that do know their God shall be strong, and do exploits. And they that understand among the people shall instruct many: yet they shall fall by the sword, and by flame, by captivity, and by spoil, many days. Now when they

shall fall, they shall be holpen with a little help: but many shall cleave to them with flatteries. And some of them of understanding shall fall, to try them, and to purge, and to make them white, even to the time of the end: because it is yet for a time appointed. (Daniel 11:32–35)

Due to the proximity of the two previous passages to the reign of Christ during the seventh trumpet and the standing up of Michael in Daniel 12:1, we may understand that both are covering the same ground, namely, seven trumpet judgments by which God prepares a people to stand during the time of the end judgment. The seventh trumpet announces that the tide has turned against Satan's stronghold over the church, and as a result of the investigative judgment (the second phase of Christ's heavenly sanctuary ministry), a clear path is opened for the Lord's return.

And the seventh angel sounded; and there were great voices in heaven, saying, The kingdoms of this world are become the kingdoms of our Lord, and of his Christ; and he shall reign for ever and ever. And the four and twenty elders, which sat before God on their seats, fell upon their faces, and worshipped God, Saying, We give thee thanks, O Lord God Almighty, which art, and wast, and art to come; because thou hast taken to thee thy great power, and hast reigned. And the nations were angry, and thy wrath is come, and the time of the dead, that they should be judged, and that thou shouldest give reward unto thy servants the prophets, and to the saints, and them that fear thy name, small and great; and shouldest destroy them which destroy the earth. And *the temple of God was opened in heaven, and there was seen in his temple the ark of his testament*: and there were lightnings, and voices, and thunderings, and an earthquake, and great hail. (Revelation 11:15–19, emphasis added)

In one breath, the seventh angel's trumpet portrays how earth's history is wrapped up by the transfer of earth's kingdoms to Jesus, judgment of the dead, and rewarding of the saints, all based on what has taken place in the Holy of Holies, where the ark of His testament is located. The history of the founding of Adventism is foretold in Revelation 10, located between the sixth and seventh trumpets, providing for us an introduction to the next phase.

Second Phase—Jesus in the Sanctuary for the Day of Atonement

Also on the tenth day of this seventh month there shall be a day of atonement: it shall be an holy convocation unto you; and ye shall afflict your souls, and offer an offering made by fire unto the LORD. And ye shall do no work in that same day: for it is a day of atonement, to make an atonement for you before the LORD your God. For whatsoever soul it be that shall not be afflicted in that same day, he shall be cut off from among his people. (Leviticus 23:27–29)

But in the days of the voice of the seventh angel, when he shall begin to sound, the mystery of God should be finished, as he hath declared to his servants the prophets. And the voice which I heard from heaven spake unto me again, and said, Go and take the little book which is open in the hand of the angel which standeth upon the sea and upon the earth. And I went unto the angel, and said unto him, Give me the little book. And he said unto me, Take it, and eat it up; and it shall make thy belly bitter, but it shall be in thy mouth sweet as honey. And I took the little book out of the angel's hand, and ate it up; and it was in my mouth sweet as honey: and as soon as I had eaten it, my belly was bitter. And he said unto me, Thou must prophesy again before many peoples, and nations, and tongues, and kings. (Revelation 10:7–11)

Those who were to "prophesy again" prophesied after the great disappointment of the 1840s, and historically, this is where Adventism comes on the scene. The next verses (11:1–13) appear to be an unbroken continuation of the previous chapter. This passage explains how the 1,260 years (twice recorded in verses 2 and 3) of papal religious and civil supremacy was actually the proving ground for developing the jewel of the Reformation—the remnant.

Although the better part of that first half of Revelation 11 is beyond our scope, the key connection for those who "prophesy again" is the "measuring" of verses 1–3:

> And there was given me a reed like unto a rod: and the angel stood, saying, Rise, and measure the temple of God, and the altar, and them that worship therein. But the court which is without the temple leave out, and measure it not; for it is given unto the Gentiles: and the holy city shall they tread under foot forty *and* two months. And I will give *power* unto my two witnesses, and they shall prophesy a thousand two hundred *and* threescore days, clothed in sackcloth.

The saints are measured during the prophesying of the two witnesses (Old and New Testaments) in sackcloth (discouraging circumstances) when they are tried and purged, falling under the fires of persecution. This lasts until the "time of the end" [end of the 1,260 years, the "time appointed" (Daniel 11:33–35)]. "That the trial of your faith, being much more precious than of gold that perisheth, though it be tried with fire, might be found unto praise and honour and glory at the appearing of Jesus Christ" (1 Peter 1:7). A large portion of the measured and faithful escaped the reach of the papal supremacy by voyaging as pilgrims to the shores of the free New World, from whence originated the beginning of the call to "prophesy again."

They prophesy in the same manner and character of Elijah in his generation. We are not far removed from entering the Elijah dimension. What propelled Elijah and his successor, John the Baptist, to prepare the way of the Lord? It would be the combination of new prophetic understanding and Christ's continuous ministry on behalf of God's flock to preserve them for deliverance when facing the perils of a looming crisis.

The second prophetic account of the remnant is found in Revelation 12 through 14, which goes on to help them understand what they are to prophesy—the Day of Atonement message, starting with the announcement "the hour of judgment has come" and featuring the "everlasting gospel." Expanding on this message was all the truth needed for surviving Satan's last desperate efforts (see Rev. 13) to disrupt the path for Christ's coming.

The remaining small flock which endured the disappointment of 1844 found, with rejoicing, that it was the Lord's purpose that a new emphasis on the second coming should go to the masses, as led by William Miller and others around the world. They confirmed a coming of Christ in 1844, but later recognized, with the help of Daniel 7 and 8 and Hebrews 8 through 10, that the location where Christ went (see Dan. 7:13–27) was the Holy of Holies in the heavenly sanctuary. In this room, containing the Ten Commandments, He began to conduct the "hour of judgment"—a fulfillment of the Day of Atonement. This would be a new phase of salvation to complete the cleansing/restoring of the congregation (see Dan. 8:13). His work there plays a further role in hastening His return to earth, as seen in the next chapter.

Early Advent Awakening—A Small-Scale Model

That bit of history, in advance of its fulfillment, is a small-scale model of what the Lord has planned for His finishing work—a movement of Jesus into the heavenly sanctuary with a corresponding revival movement on earth, purifying His people for an outpouring of spiritual rain for a rapidly completed work.

> As I presented these principles to the people in the Sabbath meeting, all seemed to feel that the Lord had spoken through the feeble instrument. We called upon those who wished to consecrate themselves to the Lord, and several responded. After these had borne their testimony, the rain came down in torrents. It seemed as if the windows of heaven were opened. I made this a symbol of what the Lord will do for his people in letting the latter rain of his rich blessing in truth and righteousness fall upon them. (White, *The Review and Herald*, April 11, 1899, par. 13)

The last trumpet alerts the saints to seek the hearing of His voice calling us to join the great advent transitioning work of Christ, the last spiritual awakening to "sanctify the congregation." Certainly, this is the one threshold-crossing fulfillment which determines the rapidity of the end—the Christ-reflecting righteousness of the church, which alone clears the way for the last conditions. The glorious finale is on hold, awaiting this one condition.

"'When the fruit is brought forth, immediately he putteth in the sickle, because the harvest is come.'" Christ is waiting with longing desire for the manifestation of Himself in His church. When the character of Christ shall be perfectly reproduced in His people, then He will come to claim them as His own." (White 1900, p. 69)

Was All Judgment Finished at the Cross?

There is a popular but detrimental theory that the judgment of all believers was completed at the cross. If that was the case, then the idea of

Christians having a role in speeding or delaying the day of God would be no more an emphasis than it was 2,000 years ago. The erroneous judgment view was developed from two apocalyptic misconceptions: preterism—Revelation's prophecies occurred approximately during the first and second centuries, and futurism—they all occur after we are secretly "raptured" to heaven. Both of these views suggest that His coming is completely arbitrary from the standpoint of any Christian involvement in aiding His coming.

> There is a popular but detrimental theory that the judgment of all believers was completed at the cross. If that was the case, then the idea of Christians having a role in speeding or delaying the day of God would be no more an emphasis than it was 2,000 years ago.

Study of the supporting evidence, however, uncovers a high degree of speculation. On the other hand, Daniel and Revelation supply convincing evidence pointing to a judgment when our books are open. This only becomes necessary just prior to the second advent when Christ brings His rewards with Him according to heaven's records (see Rev. 20:12; 22:12).

The natural tendency arising from belief that everything was finished 2,000 years ago is a humanistic desire to "live life to its fullest" and postpone, as long as possible, making a commitment to God. God's purpose is actually similar, but with a major difference: He wants us to live life to the fullest, but in the only way that it's truly possible—in hopeful anticipation of His appearing.

There was a judgment completed at the cross. "Now is the judgment of this world: now shall the prince of this world be cast out. And I, if I be lifted up from the earth, will draw all men unto me. This he said, signifying what death he should die" (John 12:31–33; see also 9:35–39; 1 John 3:8).

The subjects of this judgment were not people, but devils and the death they had brought upon humanity. The first coming of the Messiah began the restoration of humanity by accomplishing victory at the point where they had fallen, thus completing the judgment of fallen angels and invalidating their continuous accusations against His people (see Rev. 12:10).

Pre-advent Judgment Prepares the Bride for the Marriage

The following passage in Joel highlights this purifying role of the atonement judgment and ties it to the outpouring latter rain, using as its theme the marriage of a bride and bridegroom. This theme is also found in Revelation 19 and some parables of Jesus, allowing us to relate these themes to the purifying judgment.

> Therefore also now, saith the LORD, turn ye even to me with all your heart, and with fasting, and with weeping, and with mourning [This compares with the bidding of the Lord expressed to the Israelites while encamped in formation around the tabernacle on the Day of Atonement—Leviticus 23:27–29]: And rend your heart, and not your garments, and turn unto the LORD your God: for he is gracious and merciful, slow to anger, and of great kindness, and repenteth him of the evil. Who knoweth if he will return and repent, and leave a blessing behind him; even a meat offering and a drink offering unto the LORD your God? Blow the trumpet in Zion, sanctify a fast, call a solemn assembly [Recall that the trumpet sounding signaled to the people that the Day of Atonement was near—Leviticus 23:23–26]: Gather the people, sanctify the congregation, assemble the elders, gather the children, and those that suck the breasts: let the bridegroom go forth of his chamber, and the bride out of her closet.

The pre-advent judgment is an intervention that God uses to interrupt delay through a soul-stirring awakening of His people. For this reason, except for the impenitent, this judgment is not seen as a fearful, dreaded judgment, but a joyous segue to what Jesus represents as a wedding ceremony. It closes one door but opens another. It is His salvation masterpiece when the Bridegroom goes forth from His chamber (His movement to begin exiting the heavenly sanctuary) and the bride out of her closet, that His outpouring showers may fall on her citizens.

Although He didn't mention the investigative judgment directly, Jesus did reflect it in the wedding parables through a number of clues. The parables explain what takes place during that judgment by expressions similar to the language of Revelation's passages on the marriage of Jesus to New Jerusalem. "And I John saw the holy city, New Jerusalem, coming down from God out of heaven, prepared as a bride adorned for her husband" (Rev. 21:2).

> Let us be glad and rejoice, and give honour to him: for the marriage of the Lamb is come, and his wife hath made herself ready. And to her was granted that she should be arrayed in fine linen, clean and white: for the fine linen is the righteousness of saints. And he saith unto me, Write, Blessed are they which are called unto the marriage supper of the Lamb. And he saith unto me, These are the true sayings of God.... And I saw heaven opened, and behold a white horse; and he that sat upon him was called Faithful and True, and in righteousness he doth judge and make war. (Revelation 19:7–11)

Those who will experience the supreme rejoicing of living to meeting Jesus at His appearing are now being brought up to the state of fully reflecting His holiness and benevolence. This is the work of the Day of Atonement.

> Jesus sent His angels to direct the minds of the disappointed ones to the most holy place [in 1844], where He had gone to cleanse the sanctuary and make a special atonement for Israel. Jesus told the angels that all who found Him would understand the work which He was to perform. I saw that while Jesus was in the most holy place He would be married to the New Jerusalem; and after His work should be accomplished in the holiest, He would descend to the earth in kingly power and take to Himself the precious ones who had patiently waited His return. (White, *Early Writings*, p. 251)

"Gather the people, *Sanctify the congregation*, Assemble the elders, Gather the children and nursing babes; Let the bridegroom go out from his chamber, And the bride from her dressing room" (Joel 2:16, NKJV, emphasis added).

Three parables have two common themes in mind: the marriage ceremony and investigation of the guests. The Lord must have been drawing from Joel 2:16 in referring to the wedding judgment that brings together bride and bridegroom, because this judgment serves to make the bride ready (see Rev. 19:7–11 above). Once this is accomplished, the remaining time is essentially a downhill ride in terms of labor and success. The bridegroom has been ready for the bride since shortly after the wedding judgment began in 1844. As expected from the process of an investigative judgment, there is a separating and then a regathering into two, clear, decided associations—genuine and non-genuine.

> The coming of Christ as our high priest to the most holy place, for the cleansing of the sanctuary, brought to view in Daniel 8:14; the coming of the Son of man to the Ancient of Days, as presented in Daniel 7:13; and the coming of the Lord to His temple, foretold by Malachi [the refining activity of the present

hour of judgment], are descriptions of the same event; and this is also represented by the coming of the bridegroom to the marriage, described by Christ in the parable of the ten virgins, of Matthew 25. (White, *The Great Controversy*, p. 426)

First Wedding Parable—Matthew 25:1-13

Then shall the kingdom of heaven be likened unto ten virgins, which took their lamps, and went forth to meet the bridegroom. And five of them were wise, and five *were* foolish. They that *were* foolish took their lamps, and took no oil with them: But the wise took oil in their vessels with their lamps. While the bridegroom tarried, they all slumbered and slept. And at midnight there was a cry made, Behold, the bridegroom cometh; go ye out to meet him. Then all those virgins arose, and trimmed their lamps. And the foolish said unto the wise, Give us of your oil; for our lamps are gone out. But the wise answered, saying, *Not so*; lest there be not enough for us and you: but go ye rather to them that sell, and buy for yourselves. And while they went to buy, the bridegroom came; and they that were ready went in with him to the marriage: and the door was shut. Afterward came also the other virgins, saying, Lord, Lord, open to us. But he answered and said, Verily I say unto you, I know you not. Watch therefore, for ye know neither the day nor the hour wherein the Son of man cometh.

Rather than the second coming, the coming of the bridegroom here represents the outcome of the judgment, the coming of Jesus to a sanctified church via the Holy Spirit just prior to the season of refreshing/outpouring (see Acts 3:19, 20; John 14:16–18).

The coming of the bridegroom, here brought to view, takes place before the marriage. The marriage represents the reception by Christ of His kingdom. The Holy City, the New Jerusalem, which is the capital and representative of the kingdom, is called "the bride, the Lamb's wife." Said the angel to John: "Come hither, I will show thee the bride, the Lamb's wife." "He carried me away in the spirit," says the prophet, "and showed me that great city, the holy Jerusalem, descending out of heaven from God." Revelation 21:9, 10. Clearly, then, the bride represents the Holy City, and the virgins that go out to meet the bridegroom are a symbol of the church. In the Revelation the people of God are said to be the guests at the marriage supper. Revelation 19:9. If *guests*, they cannot be represented also as the *bride*. Christ, as stated by the prophet Daniel, will receive from the Ancient of Days in heaven, "dominion, and glory, and a kingdom;" He will receive the New Jerusalem, the capital of His kingdom, "prepared as a bride adorned for her husband." Daniel 7:14; Revelation 21:2. Having received the kingdom, He will come in His glory, as King of kings and Lord of lords, for the redemption of His people, who are to "sit down with Abraham, and Isaac, and Jacob," at His table in His kingdom (Matthew 8:11; Luke 22:30), to partake of the marriage supper of the Lamb. (White, *The Great Controversy*, p. 426–427)

Distinguished from the bride, the guests in any case become the citizens of the bride, characterized by the same fine linen of the bride, "clean and white: for the fine linen is the righteousness of saints" (Rev. 19:8). "And the nations of them which are saved shall walk in the light of it [the bride]: and the kings of the earth do bring their glory and honour into it" (Rev. 21:24).

> As Christ sat looking upon the party that waited for the bridegroom, He told His disciples the story of the ten virgins, by their experience *illustrating the experience of the church that shall live just before His Second Coming.*
>
> The two classes of watchers represent the two classes who profess to be waiting for their Lord. They are called virgins because they profess a pure faith. By the lamps is represented the word of God. The psalmist says, "Thy word is a lamp unto my feet, and a light unto may path." (White, *Christ's Object Lessons*, p. 406, emphasis added)

The parable, in more depth, highlights the gift, His Spirit (the oil), that enables the lamp of His Word to burn.

> In the parable, all the ten virgins went out to meet the bridegroom. All had lamps and vessels for oil. For a time there was seen no difference between them. So with the church that lives just before Christ's second coming. All have a knowledge of the Scriptures. All have heard the message of Christ's near approach, and confidently expect His appearing. But as in the parable, so it is now. A time of waiting intervenes, faith is tried; and when the cry is heard, "Behold, the Bridegroom cometh; go ye out to meet Him," many are unready. They have no oil in their vessels with their lamps. They are destitute of the Holy Spirit. (White, *Christ's Object Lessons*, p. 408)

> In the parable it was those that had oil in their vessels with their lamps that went in to the marriage. Those who, with a knowledge of the truth from the Scriptures, had also the Spirit and grace of God, and who, in the night of their bitter trial, had patiently waited, searching the Bible for clearer light— these saw the truth concerning the sanctuary in heaven and the

> Saviour's change in ministration, and by faith they followed Him in His work in the sanctuary above. And all who through the testimony of the Scriptures accept the same truths, following Christ by faith as He enters in before God to perform the last work of mediation, and at its close to receive His kingdom—all these are represented as going in to the marriage. (White, *The Great Controversy*, p. 427–428)

What would cause church members to think that Christ is about to return while they are still living? This is evidenced by their awakening and immediately setting out to trim their lamps (prayerfully study the Word). Perhaps they heard the worldwide announcement of peace and safety. "For when they shall say, Peace and safety; then sudden destruction cometh upon them, as travail upon a woman with child; and they shall not escape" (1 Thess. 5:3).

> It is in a crisis that character is revealed. When the earnest voice proclaimed at midnight, "Behold, the bridegroom cometh; go ye out to meet him," and the sleeping virgins were roused from their slumbers, it was seen who had made preparation for the event. Both parties were taken unawares; but one was prepared for the emergency, and the other was found without preparation. So now, a sudden and unlooked-for calamity, something that brings the soul face to face with death, will show whether there is any real faith in the promises of God. It will show whether the soul is sustained by grace. (White, *Christ's Object Lessons*, p. 412)

This compares well with the picture presented in Daniel 11:45–12:1: "And he [papal power] shall plant the tabernacles of his palace between the seas in the glorious holy mountain; yet he shall come to his end, and none shall help him. And at that time shall Michael stand up, the great prince which standeth for the children of thy people: and there shall be a time of trouble, such as never was since there was a nation even to that same time: and at that time thy people shall be delivered, every one that shall be found written in the book."

The following quotations combine elements from both the first and third parables:

> Let none follow the example of the foolish virgins and think that it will be safe to wait until the crisis comes before gaining a preparation of character to stand in that time. It will be too late to seek for the righteousness of Christ when the guests are called in and examined. Now is the time to put on the righteousness of Christ—the wedding garment that will fit you to enter into the marriage supper of the Lamb. (White, *That I May Know Him*, p. 350)

> Because of their neglect the Lord has looked with disfavor upon the church. A love of ease and selfish indulgence has been shown by many. Some who have had the privilege of knowing Bible truth have not brought it into the inner sanctuary of the soul. God holds all these accountable for the talents which they have not returned to Him in honest, faithful service in making every effort possible to seek and to save those who were lost. These slothful servants are represented as coming to the wedding supper without the wedding garment, the robe of the righteousness of Christ. They have nominally accepted the truth, but they do not practice it. Professedly circumcised, they are in reality among the uncircumcised. (White, *Testimonies for the Church*, vol. 6, pp. 295–296)

The proclamation, "Behold, the Bridegroom cometh," in the summer of 1844, led thousands to expect the immediate advent of the Lord. At the appointed time the Bridegroom came, not to the earth, as the people expected, but to the Ancient of Days in heaven, to the marriage, the reception of His kingdom. "They that were ready went in with Him to the marriage: and the door was shut." They were not to be present in person at the marriage; for it takes place in heaven, while they are upon the earth. The followers of Christ are to "wait for their Lord, when He will *return from* the wedding." Luke 12:36. But they are to understand His work, and to follow Him by faith as He goes in before God. It is in this sense that they are said to go in to the marriage. (White, *The Great Controversy*, p. 427)

The awakening of the mid-1800s prepared the way for the announcement of the bridegroom, coming at the beginning of the investigative judgment, when a door opened for earnest believers to participate by faith in this new ministry of Christ in the sanctuary's Most Holy Place. There He began performing heaven's wedding ceremony.

It is those who by faith follow Jesus in the great work of the atonement who receive the benefits of His mediation in their behalf, while those who reject the light which brings to view this work of ministration are not benefitted thereby. The Jews who rejected the light given at Christ's first advent, and refused to believe on Him as the Saviour of the world, could not receive pardon through Him. When Jesus at His ascension entered by His own blood into the heavenly sanctuary to shed upon His disciples the blessings of His mediation, the Jews were left in total darkness to continue their useless sacrifices and offerings. The ministration of types and shadows had ceased. That door by which men had formerly found access to God was no longer open. (White, *The Great Controversy*, p. 430)

Likewise, the door for access to God during the 1,800 years after Jesus ascended was no longer open when Jesus opened the inner door of the sanctuary in 1844 to sanctify the bride.

The Day of Atonement judgment gives the wise wedding guests a fitness for the last feast fulfillment—Tabernacles.

This is the message of the second wedding parable, in two parts. The first part describes the character of those who enter the wedding ceremony: humility, compassion, and undivided devotion.

Second Wedding Parable—Luke 14:7-24

> And he put forth a parable to those which were bidden, when he marked how they chose out the chief rooms; saying unto them, When thou art bidden of any *man* to a wedding, sit not down in the highest room; lest a more honourable man than thou be bidden of him; And he that bade thee and him come and say to thee, Give this man place; and thou begin with shame to take the lowest room. But when thou art bidden, go and sit down in the lowest room; that when he that bade thee cometh, he may say unto thee, Friend, go up higher: then shalt thou have worship in the presence of them that sit at meat with thee. For whosoever exalteth himself shall be abased; and he that humbleth himself shall be exalted. Then said he also to him that bade him, When thou makest a dinner or a supper, call not thy friends, nor thy brethren, neither thy kinsmen, nor *thy* rich neighbours; lest they also bid thee again, and a recompense be made thee. But when thou makest a feast, call the poor, the maimed, the lame, the blind: And thou shalt be blessed; for they cannot recompense thee: for thou shalt be recompensed at the resurrection of the just. And when one of them that sat at meat with him heard these things, he said unto him, Blessed

is he that shall eat bread in the kingdom of God. Then said he unto him, A certain man made a great supper, and bade many: And sent his servant at supper time to say to them that were bidden, Come; for all things are now ready. And they all with one *consent* began to make excuse. The first said unto him, I have bought a piece of ground, and I must needs go and see it: I pray thee have me excused. And another said, I have bought five yoke of oxen, and I go to prove them: I pray thee have me excused. And another said, I have married a wife, and therefore I cannot come. So that servant came, and shewed his lord these things. Then the master of the house being angry said to his servant, Go out quickly into the streets and lanes of the city, and bring in hither the poor, and the maimed, and the halt, and the blind. And the servant said, Lord, it is done as thou hast commanded, and yet there is room. And the lord said unto the servant, Go out into the highways and hedges, and compel *them* to come in, that my house may be filled. For I say unto you, That none of those men which were bidden shall taste of my supper.

The call to go out to the highways and byways is equivalent to the harvest-ready fruit of the parable of Mark 4:26–29.

In the last words of Jesus before ascending—"But ye shall receive power, after that the Holy Ghost is come upon you: and ye shall be witnesses unto me both in Jerusalem, and in all Judaea, and in Samaria, and unto the uttermost part of the earth" (Acts 1:8)—do the highways and byways corresponds with the uttermost part of the earth? The highways lead to city dwellers and the byways/hedges lead to the country dwellers. The third and fourth tasks are closely bound during that last outpouring—the filling of His house follows on the heels of the global gospel sounding.

As it pertains to the annual holy feast day types, Acts 1:8 is dualistic in applying to both the first apostles and end-time apostles, with a corresponding first and end-time Pentecost (which is Tabernacles). The highways-and-byways command corresponds also with the parable of the eleventh-hour workers who are the last ones before the final harvest (see Matt. 20:6–8). Are we not in the eleventh hour today? And could the world require more people than are now on the earth to provide the gathering that fills God's house?

"Herein is my Father glorified, that ye bear much fruit; so shall ye be my disciples" (John 15:8). As soon as the twelve became ripened disciples in His likeness, then they received power to bear much fruit. Multitudes immediately noticed and recognized this activity as a genuine movement of God; so also will the church today be surprised to find public interest generated over her message, when accompanied by new power from above.

Mark 4 and Luke 14 don't explicitly connect the rain with the wedding and fruit bearing; but again, Joel makes this connection. In Joel 2:15,16, and 23, after the bride and bridegroom appear, what is the effect of the last rains? The next verse metaphorically declares the outcome—the last condition for Christ's coming and the filling of His house. "And the floors shall be full of wheat, and the vats shall overflow with wine and oil" (v. 24).

Third Wedding Parable—Matt. 22:1-14

An important difference between entering the door to meet the bridegroom of the first parable and entering the wedding feast of the second and third parables is that the guests of the latter two are still waiting for the bridegroom. He comes when the hall is filled and the guests of the second parable (Luke 14) fill the hall after being gathered by the last-hour servants (Matt. 20:1–8).

After a lengthy struggle to get enough people interested in the king's wedding invitation, there is finally success—a hall full of guests. It would be convenient if the story ended here, but one simple qualification remains.

> And Jesus answered and spake unto them again by parables, and said, The kingdom of heaven is like unto a certain king, which made a marriage for his son, And sent forth his servants to call them that were bidden to the wedding: and they would not come. Again, he sent forth other servants, saying, Tell them which are bidden, Behold, I have prepared my dinner: my oxen and my fatlings are killed, and all things are ready: come unto the marriage. But they made light of it, and went their ways, one to his farm, another to his merchandise: And the remnant took his servants, and entreated them spitefully, and slew them. But when the king heard thereof, he was wroth: and he sent forth his armies, and destroyed those murderers, and burned up their city. Then saith he to his servants, The wedding is ready, but they which were bidden were not worthy. Go ye therefore into the highways, and as many as ye shall find, bid to the marriage. So those servants went out into the highways, and gathered together all as many as they found, both bad and good: and the wedding was furnished with guests. (Matthew 22:1–10)

Both the wedding and dinner in the parable were prepared together, a universal custom until now. Then the call was made for the invitees, who plainly and without cause responded by showing contempt against the king and his son. After armies burned their city, there was a second wedding announcement, inasmuch as there is a second call for more guests and a second Israel who gives the call (see 21:43).

As the next verses of the parable show, merely being admitted to the wedding did not guarantee being selected as an official attendee. The king gave a simple test to assure that the wedding would not be spoiled: Just come in wearing the royal apparel supplied in advance by the king. The sanctuary pre-advent judgment accomplishes the remnant's second goal, providing the clean garment of Christ through daily faith—a light burden. Praise His name (Rom. 13:14; Matt. 11:30; Rev. 19:7, 8; Isa. 61:10)!

> And when the king came in to see the guests, he saw there a man which had not on a wedding garment: And he saith unto him, Friend, how camest thou in hither not having a wedding garment? And he was speechless. Then said the king to the servants, Bind him hand and foot, and take him away, and cast him into outer darkness; there shall be weeping and gnashing of teeth. For many are called, but few are chosen. (Matthew 22:11–14)

That outer darkness is not yet the lake of fire, but spiritual darkness—disconnection from the Spirit and not receiving rain; therefore not sealed.

"The parable of the wedding garment opens before us a lesson of the highest consequence. By the marriage is represented the union of humanity with divinity; the wedding garment represents the character which all must possess who shall be accounted fit guests for the wedding" (White 1900, p. 307). From the beginning of this parable, the invitation is understood to have begun with the nation of Israel when Jesus was yet with them. True to the parable, the messengers of the Lord have been entreated spitefully and slain up until the end of the 1700s, followed by the brief reprieve of the last couple hundred years. Only when the persecution of the reformers ended could the invitation to the highways be fully realized.

> We are living in a time when the last message of mercy, the last invitation, is sounding to the children of men. The command,

"Go out into the highways and hedges," is reaching its final fulfillment. To every soul Christ's invitation will be given. The messengers are saying, "Come; for all things are now ready." Heavenly angels are still working in co-operation with human agencies. The Holy Spirit is presenting every inducement to constrain you to come. Christ is watching for some sign that will betoken the removing of the bolts and the opening of the door of your heart for His entrance. Angels are waiting to bear the tidings to heaven that another lost sinner has been found. The hosts of heaven are waiting, ready to strike their harps and to sing a song of rejoicing that another soul has accepted the invitation to the gospel feast. (White, *Christ's Object Lessons*, p. 237)

While the wedding hall is still filling, the investigating that will complete the bride's preparation for the wedding and supper continues until she becomes His wife.

In the parable of Matthew 22 the same figure of the marriage is introduced, and the investigative judgment is clearly represented as taking place before the marriage. Previous to the wedding the king comes in to see the guests, to see if all are attired in the wedding garment, the spotless robe of character washed and made white in the blood of the Lamb. Matthew 22:11; Revelation 7:14. He who is found wanting is cast out, but all who upon examination are seen to have the wedding garment on are accepted of God and accounted worthy of a share in His kingdom and a seat upon His throne. This work of examination of character, of determining who are prepared for the kingdom of God, is that of the investigative judgment, the closing of work in the sanctuary above. (White, *The Great Controversy*, p. 428)

An important difference exists between this wedding and a typical one with respect to the guests. Instead of witnesses of the bride and groom, the guests are collectively citizens of the "bride." Even in this world, the guests have a sense of being one family with the bride and groom, even though they may not all be related. When the wedding guests are all in place, then the wedding may commence, bringing us to the next festival shadow fulfillment—Tabernacles.

> When the work of investigation shall be ended, when the cases of those who in all ages have professed to be followers of Christ have been examined and decided, then, and not till then, probation will close, and the door of mercy will be shut. Thus in the one short sentence, "They that were ready went in with Him to the marriage: and the door was shut," we are carried down through the Saviour's final ministration, to the time when the great work for man's salvation shall be completed. (White, *The Great Controversy*, p. 428)

There is an initial door closing and a final door closing (see 1 Peter 4:17 and Rev. 22:11, 12). The reality that guests have entered the wedding banquet still to be inspected speaks of an earlier probation, followed by a global, culminating probation. To complete the filling of the hall with guests, God's finishing touch is to pour out His rain—the unrestrained Spirit baptism—for gathering and clothing the scattered saints. Then the congregation is formed, which completes New Jerusalem. Then, at that point, investigation is no longer conducted. Revelation 19 represents a church that is married, no longer only a bride; "His wife has made herself ready" with the white linen garment, the righteousness of the saints by grace. Heaven's wedding guest investigation is the compelling of church members to set the Lord always before them. Because he is at their right hand, they shall not be moved. (Ps. 16:8)

The Personal Effect of This Judgment for Hastening Christ

Since the heart of humanity's restoration is righteousness/salvation by grace through faith (see Eph. 2:8), this is the foundation for reaching for what lies ahead, the finishing touch upon His people so they may prepare the way of the Lord, making His path straight (see Luke 3:4). Assuming that the reader is anchored in the doctrine and baptism of faith, we can then approach the question of what effect the pre-advent judgment has on imputing to us the level of righteousness through faith that corresponds with moving forward the day of God.

There is a definite difference of expectation when comparing Christian life before the Day of Atonement judgment and Christian life after it began. Recalling from Acts 3:21, Jesus remains in heaven "until the times of restitution of all things." This judgment, at the opening of heaven's books (see Daniel 7:10), invokes the highest level of righteousness through confession, repentance, and blotting out of sins, characterized as restitution, a restoration of all that recognizes the original image of God in humankind. "Elias truly shall first come, and restore all things" (Matt. 17:11). Elijah so represented this restoration that he could no longer remain on earth; he represents all who are translated when Christ appears.

The opening of heaven's books after 1844 indicates a recording of progress towards the restoration goal. The pre-advent judgment, as a hastening role of God, minimizes delay by providing the congregation greater vigilance with temptation, knowing that we have pages dedicated to us in heaven's books, yet drawing encouragement from this due to the greater sense of dwelling in the personal presence of Jesus, beholding His ongoing high-priestly ministry on our behalf. Here, the record books of our lives are under His direct solicitude. "Neither is there any creature that is not manifest in his sight: but all things are naked and opened unto the eyes of him with whom we have to do. Seeing then that we have a great high priest, that is passed into the heavens, Jesus the Son of God, let us hold fast our profession" (Heb. 4:13, 14).

> Well, suppose you are walking in the light, what then? Why, your testimonies will be light. You will talk light, and all this evil surmising and evil speaking will be put away. You will talk and we will not be thinking of ourselves and what others are doing, but what God and Jesus are doing. Well, what are they doing? They are cleansing the sanctuary. Well, we should be with Him in this work and be cleansing the sanctuary of our souls of all unrighteousness, that our names may [be] written in the Lamb's book of life, that our sins may be blotted out when the times of refreshing shall come from the presence of the Lord. It is the most solemn work that was ever given to mortals. (White, *The Ellen G. White 1888 Materials*, p. 161)

> The cases of all will be brought up in the judgment and if their sins are not confessed their names will then be blotted from the book of life, and their lot will be with the adulterers and the fornicators, and deceivers, and those who love and make a lie. "Thou hast a few names even in Sardis which have not defiled their garments; and they shall walk with me in white: for they are worthy. He that overcometh, the same shall be clothed in white raiment: and I will not blot out his name out of the book of life, but I will confess his name before my Father, and before His angels" ([Revelation 3:]4, 5). (White, *Manuscript Releases*, vol. 10, p. 267)

With this awareness comes solemnity of the occasion and the infinite value placed on their wedding guest invitations. This awareness produces one of two responses, depending on whether the daily wedding garment is being put on according to the first angel's message. Eventually, the effect of bringing this judgment awareness to the fore is a sifting of the chaff from the wheat. "I indeed baptize you with water unto repentance: but he that cometh after me is mightier than I, whose shoes I am not worthy to bear: he shall baptize you with the Holy Ghost, and *with* fire: Whose fan *is* in his hand, and he will thoroughly purge his floor, and gather his wheat into the garner; but he will burn up the chaff with unquenchable fire" (Matt. 3:11, 12).

Restoration Level of Righteousness by Faith

"But we are bound to give thanks alway to God for you, brethren beloved of the Lord, because God hath from the beginning chosen you to salvation through sanctification of the Spirit and belief of the truth" (2 Thess. 2:13).

Daily, "If you give yourself to Him, and accept Him as your Saviour, then, sinful as your life may have been, for His sake you are accounted righteous. Christ's character stands in place of your character, and you are accepted before God just as if you had not sinned" (White 1892, p. 62).

> If the heart has been renewed by the Spirit of God, the life will bear witness to the fact. While we cannot do anything to change our hearts or to bring ourselves into harmony with God; while we must not trust at all to ourselves or our good works, our lives will reveal whether the grace of God is dwelling within us. A change will be seen in the character, the habits, the pursuits. The contrast will be clear and decided between what they have been and what they are. (White, *Steps to Christ*, p. 57)

> The germination of the seed represents the beginning of spiritual life, and the development of the plant is a beautiful figure of Christian growth. As in nature, so in grace; there can be no

life without growth. The plant must either grow or die. As its growth is silent and imperceptible, but continuous, so is the development of the Christian life. At every stage of development our life may be perfect; yet if God's purpose for us is fulfilled, there will be continual advancement. Sanctification is the work of a lifetime. As our opportunities multiply, our experience will enlarge, and our knowledge increase. We shall become strong to bear responsibility, and our maturity will be in proportion to our privileges.

The plant grows by receiving that which God has provided to sustain its life. It sends down its roots into the earth. It drinks in the sunshine, the dew, and the rain. It receives the life-giving properties from the air. So the Christian is to grow by co-operating with the divine agencies. Feeling our helplessness, we are to improve all the opportunities granted us to gain a fuller experience. As the plant takes root in the soil, so we are to take deep root in Christ. As the plant receives the sunshine, the dew, and the rain, we are to open our hearts to the Holy Spirit. The work is to be done "not by might, nor by power, but by My Spirit, saith the Lord of hosts." Zechariah 4:6. *If we keep our minds stayed upon Christ, He will come unto us "as the rain, as the latter and former rain unto the earth."* Hosea 6:3. As the Sun of Righteousness, He will arise upon us "with healing in His wings." Malachi 4:2. We shall "grow as the lily." We shall "revive as the corn, and grow as the vine." Hosea 14:5, 7. By constantly relying upon Christ as our personal Saviour, we shall grow up into Him in all things who is our head." (White, *Christ's Object Lessons*, pp. 65–67, emphasis added)

The clause "At every stage of development our life may be perfect" may sound contradictory to righteousness by faith, but a perfect life to Ellen White and the Scriptures is the credit given to the sinner having *perfect faith* in Jesus Christ, fulfilling in him the righteousness of God's law (see Rom. 8:3, 4). "For by one offering he hath perfected for ever them that are sanctified" (Heb. 10:14). Through His offering, we are counted as perfected, though in real time, we may still often succumb to sin. Through repentance, the offering of His perfection on our behalf remains.

In harmony with this, Ellen White, in *Steps to Christ*, gives the basis for how our characters are measured. "The character is revealed, not by occasional good deeds and occasional misdeeds, but by the tendency of the habitual words and acts" (pp. 57, 58). Just prior to that, she differentiates the righteousness of humanity and that imparted by faith.

> The conscience can be freed from condemnation. Through faith in His blood, all may be made perfect in Christ Jesus. Thank God that we are not dealing with impossibilities. We may claim sanctification. We may enjoy the favor of God. We are not to be anxious about what Christ and God think of us, but about what God thinks of Christ, our Substitute. (White, *Selected Messages*, book 2, pp. 32–33).

> By His perfect obedience He has made it possible for every human being to obey God's commandments. When we submit ourselves to Christ, the heart is united with His heart, the will is merged in His will, the mind becomes one with His mind, the thoughts are brought into captivity to Him; we live His life. This is what it means to be clothed with the garment of His righteousness. Then as the Lord looks upon us He sees, not the fig-leaf garment, not the nakedness and deformity of sin, but His own robe of righteousness, which is perfect obedience to the law of Jehovah. (White, *Maranatha*, p. 225)

Yet in this life, no human will be able to claim to be without sin and therefore no longer a sinner. "If we say that we have no sin, we deceive ourselves, and the truth is not in us" (1 John 1:8). The idea has come to many that only a state of sinlessness is acceptable during the judgment. While we cannot arrive at a place of claiming sinlessness, we may exercise perfect faith, the unwavering faith of a child, by which God declares us perfect through the perfect life of His Son covering us.

The Apostle Paul states that he has not attained, but "forgetting those things which are behind [past sins], and reaching forth unto those things which are before, I press toward the mark for the prize of the high calling of God in Christ Jesus" (Phil. 3:13, 14). It is with this thought that Peter prompts the Christians of the last days to "grow in the grace and knowledge of our Lord and Savior Jesus Christ" (2 Peter 3:18, NKJV) and furthermore, over the long haul of our earthly lifetime. "You do not at one bound reach perfection; sanctification is the work of a lifetime" (White 1980, p. 193).

Scripture definitely recognizes the need for ongoing forgiveness for unintended sins like losing temper in traffic, a slip of the tongue, etc. (see 1 John 1:8–2:2). However, when it comes to the would-be last generation, something new must take place to assure that their hearts remain clean when He appears. I think most Adventist Christians are in agreement that believers will not sin after the close of probation when the Revelation 22:11 announcement is made: "he that is righteous, let him be righteous still" and so on. This is connected to the midnight cry of Matthew 25:6: "Behold, the bridegroom cometh; go ye out to meet Him." At some point during the days leading up to the close of probation, by grace they would have already stopped sinning, even by thought, otherwise they could not be sealed when the winds of strife are loosed and there is no longer a mediator.

Do they resolve to stop sinning when they come to realize that the time of trouble is closing in? We know from Scripture that to stop sinning by will power alone is an impossibility. In actuality, what is closer to the truth is that they stop sinning without being aware of it because their focus is on an unbroken beholding of and communion/fellowship with Christ—the

Elijah/Enoch level of faith through which they become transformed to fully reflect God's image. This is the appeal of Revelation 3:20–21—that for the last of the seven churches, Jesus is knocking at the entrance, that the overcoming life of communion with God may be imparted.

This restored character of the church is portrayed by Peter here:

> According as his divine power hath given unto us all things that pertain unto life and godliness, through the knowledge of him that hath called us to glory and virtue: Whereby are given unto us exceeding great and precious promises: that by these ye might be partakers of the divine nature, having escaped the corruption that is in the world through lust. And beside this, giving all diligence, add to your faith virtue; and to virtue knowledge; And to knowledge temperance; and to temperance patience; and to patience godliness; And to godliness brotherly kindness; and to brotherly kindness charity. (2 Peter 1:3–7)

The capstones of reflecting Christ are the last two items of verse 7—brotherly love and *agape* love (see Matt. 22:37–40). "And above all these things put on charity [Greek *agape*], which is the bond of perfectness" (Col. 3:14). These are faith levels that are acquired through the spiritual dews and rains. The sixth church of Revelation 3 describes the remnant at the close, both in terms of their ultimate character manifested in love for people and supreme love for God.

The name of the sixth Church, Philadelphia, means "brotherly love," the same Greek word as the term "brotherly kindness" in 2 Peter 1:7.

The evidence of a sanctified congregation is unity of love for one another, answering the prayer of Jesus in John 17, that they would be one, meaning there is no longer any grudge-holding, strife, or contentions. "There is nothing that Christ hungers and thirsts for so much as whole-hearted disciples, possessing his love and gentleness" (White 1987, p. 1482).

Christ prayed that His disciples might be one as He was one with the Father. This unity is the credentials of Christ to the world that God sent Him. When self-will is renounced in reference to matters there will be a union of believers with Christ. This all should pray for and work for determinedly, thus answering as far as possible the prayer of Christ for unity in His church. (White, *Testimonies for the Church*, vol. 5, p. 94)

Abiding in Christ Level of Righteousness by Faith

"Abide in me, and I in you. As the branch cannot bear fruit of itself, except it abide in the vine; no more can ye, except ye abide in me" (John 15:4).

"Abiding in Christ is choosing only the disposition of Christ, so that his interests are identified with yours. Abide in him, to be and to do only what he wills. These are the conditions of discipleship, and unless they are complied with, you can never find rest. Rest is in Christ; it cannot be as something apart from him" (White 1958, p. 110).

After appointed worship times, the tendency is to section these off as separate from our next pursuit—where we left off in daily affairs; but a goal of faith is the blending of the two.

> *After appointed worship times, the tendency is to section these off as separate from our next pursuit—where we left off in daily affairs; but a goal of faith is the blending of the two.*

We may have long followed the narrow path, but it is not safe to take this as proof that we shall follow it to the end. If we have walked with God in fellowship of the Spirit, it is because we have sought Him daily by faith. From the two olive trees the golden oil flowing through the

> golden pipes has been communicated to us. But those who do not cultivate the spirit and habit of prayer cannot expect to receive the golden oil of goodness, patience, long-suffering, gentleness, love.
>
> Everyone is to keep himself separate from the world, which is full of iniquity. We are not to walk with God for a time, and then part from His company and walk in the sparks of our own kindling. There must be a firm continuance, a perseverance in acts of faith. We are to praise God; to show forth His glory in a righteous character. No one of us will gain the victory without persevering, untiring effort, proportionate to the value of the object which we seek, even eternal life. (White, *Testimonies to Ministers and Gospel Workers*, p. 511)

Under what conditions may the showers of God's rain be sent as a promise to claim in prayer?

> When the laborers have an abiding Christ in their own souls, when all selfishness is dead, when there is no rivalry, no strife for the supremacy, when oneness exists, when they sanctify themselves, so that love for one another is seen and felt, *then the showers of the grace of the Holy Spirit will just as surely come upon them as that God's promise will never fail in one jot or tittle*. But when the work of others is discounted, that the workers may show their own superiority, they prove that their own work does not bear the signature it should God cannot bless them. (White, *Last Day Events*, p. 190)

At a time of great moral perils, when the spread of evil is reaching new depths, an abiding level of consecration is our safeguard and path to spiritual power, dispelling every distress of darkness. "If ye abide in me, and my words abide in you, ye shall ask what ye will, and it shall be done unto you" (John 15:7). The delight of abiding in God is just a step from communion with Him.

Communion Level of Righteousness of Faith

"I will bless the LORD who has given me counsel; My heart also instructs me in the night seasons. I have set the LORD always before me; Because *He is* at my right hand I shall not be moved" (Psalm 16:7, 8, NKJV). Though at times, heaven may seem to be quiet, abiding in Christ will assure us that His voice will not be missed or resisted when He speaks to us. "I will stand upon my watch, and set me upon the tower, and will watch to see what he will say unto me, and what I shall answer when I am reproved" (Hab. 2:1).

What makes abiding in and communion with Christ a deeper level of righteousness? This echoes back to humanity's original unfallen design. "Adam, in his innocence had enjoyed open communion with His Maker" (White 1890, p. 67). After Adam and Eve settled into life after the fall, the worst devastation was not the fear of death, but the loss of open fellowship with their Creator. (This loss is what took Jesus' life on our behalf.) Afterwards, when they desired to have this fellowship back, they were sustained by the hope of restoration through the promise of a coming Deliverer (see Gen. 3:15). Without this, they could only think of how they could ever face Jesus again (because of their guilt). Through the ages until now, without the gospel, this has continued to be the main mental affliction of humanity. Then sanctification through repentance, born of faith in the slain Lamb of God, becomes the vital turning point, restoring open fellowship with our Maker.

To gain an idea of how valuable this restoration is, consider what it cost Jesus to reconcile us back to Him—leaving the throne room of the universe, condescending to our lowly stature for about thirty-three years, and then having no escape from tasting the penalty of sin, the death that we deserved. "Looking unto Jesus the author and finisher of our faith; who for the joy that was set before him endured the cross, despising the shame, and is set down at the right hand of the throne of God" (Heb. 12:2). That joy was turning the tide of humanity back to open communion with our Maker.

Looking back at the original Day of Atonement for ancient Israel, the assignment for the people was to set aside this day for soul affliction. "For on that day shall the priest make an atonement for you, to cleanse you, that ye may be clean from all your sins before the LORD. It shall be a sabbath of rest unto you, and ye shall afflict your souls, by a statute for ever" (Lev. 16:30, 31). How could such a seemingly unpleasant exercise as soul affliction correspond to communion with God? Could this be an emphasis on works? The original meaning of the word "affliction" from the Hebrew is "shrieking" or "crying out." In light of this, affliction of soul is really a prayer of faith on the level of Jacob wrestling with God. "I will not let thee go, except thou bless me." (Genesis 33:26).

"For He hath not despised nor abhorred the affliction of the afflicted; neither hath he hid his face from him; but when he cried unto him, he heard" (Ps. 22:24). Establishing a two-way encounter with God (as well as fellowship with unfallen worlds) is really the goal of the Day of Atonement.

> The whole ceremony was designed to impress the Israelites with the holiness of God and His abhorrence of sin; and, further, to show them that they could not come in contact with sin without becoming polluted. Every man was required to afflict his soul while this work of atonement was going forward. All business was to be laid aside, and the whole congregation of Israel were to spend the day in solemn humiliation before God, with prayer, fasting, and deep searching of heart. (White, *The Great Controversy*, pp. 419–420)

> The Jews had refused to seek Him in the only way whereby He could then be found, through the ministration in the sanctuary in heaven. Therefore they found no communion with God. To them the door was shut. They had no knowledge of Christ as the true sacrifice and the only mediator before God; hence they could not receive the benefits of His mediation. (White, *The Great Controversy*, p. 430)

> The class represented by the foolish virgins are not hypocrites. They have a regard for the truth, they have advocated the truth, they are attracted to those who believe the truth; but they have not yielded themselves to the Holy Spirit's working. They have not fallen upon the Rock, Christ Jesus, and permitted their old nature to be broken up. This class are represented also by the stony-ground hearers. They receive the word with readiness, but they fail of assimilating its principles. Its influence is not abiding. The Spirit works upon man's heart, according to his desire and consent implanting in him a new nature; but the class represented by the foolish virgins have been content with a superficial work. They do not know God. They have not studied His character; they have not held communion with Him; therefore they do not know how to trust, how to look and live. (White, *Christ's Object Lessons*, p. 411)

Could the essence of sanctification for the last generation be the taking in of the daily dews that produce a sin-washed, two-way communion with God? It would be the Enoch/Elijah moment, and for a united people, the point of crossing over the threshold to eternity.

> "Blessed are the pure in heart: for they shall see God." For three hundred years Enoch had been seeking purity of heart, that he might be in harmony with heaven. For three centuries

he had walked with God. Day by day he had longed for a closer union; nearer and nearer had grown the communion, until God took him to Himself. He had stood at the threshold of the eternal world, only a step between him and the land of the blest; and now the portals opened, the walk with God, so long pursued on earth, continued, and he passed through the gates of the holy city, the first from among men to enter there....

To such communion God is calling us. As was Enoch's must be their holiness of character who shall be redeemed from among men at the Lord's second coming. (White, *Maranatha*, p. 65, emphasis added)

Here the experience of Enoch is comparable with the 144,000 who are "redeemed from among men" (Rev. 14:4)—the last generation.

To His faithful followers Christ has been a daily companion and familiar friend. They have lived in close contact, in constant communion with God. Upon them the glory of the Lord has risen. In them the light of the knowledge of the glory of God in the face of Jesus Christ has been reflected. Now they rejoice in the undimmed rays of the brightness and glory of the King in His majesty. They are prepared for the communion of heaven; for they have heaven in their hearts. (White, *Christ's Object Lessons*, p. 421)

Communion with Christ—how unspeakably precious! Such communion it is our privilege to enjoy if we will seek it, if we will make any sacrifice to secure it. When the early disciples heard the words of Christ, they felt their need of Him. They sought, they found, they followed Him. They were with Him in the house, at the table, in the closet, in the field. They were with Him as pupils with a teacher, daily receiving from His lips

> lessons of holy truth. They looked to Him as servants to their master, to learn their duty. They served Him cheerfully, gladly. They followed Him, as soldiers follow their commander, fighting the good fight of faith. "And they that are with Him are called, and chosen, and faithful." (White, *Testimonies for the Church*, vol. 5, p. 223)

How is this communion realized? Scripture provides many "visual aids;" among these are Isaiah 41:10–13, expressing this faith as taking His right hand with our right hand. Then there's Revelation 3:20: "I stand at the door, and knock: if any man hear my voice, and open the door, I will come in to him, and will sup with him, and he with me." This is the invitation to the wedding supper.

The apostles spent three years hearing and seeing God. Like the accused woman thrown before Jesus (John 8), Peter's value of the invitation was traced to his most cherished memory, being rescued at his lowest moment. He well knew what Jesus was saying at that instant. Later, instead of losing his apostleship, the Lord fully restored His friend.

> Then the disciple remembered the words which Jesus had spoken to him in the upper chamber, and also his own zealous assertion, "Though all men shall be offended because of Thee, yet will I never be offended." Matthew 26:33. He had denied his Lord, even with cursing and swearing; but that look of Jesus' melted Peter's heart and saved him. He wept bitterly and repented of his great sin, and was converted, and then was prepared to strengthen his brethren. (White, *The Story of Redemption*, pp. 213–214)

What other expressions does the Bible provide with respect to hearing God speak and beholding Him by faith? See Psalms 29:2–3; 123:2; Proverbs 1:23, 33; 8:34; Isaiah 1:18; (beware of counterfeits—Isa. 8:20; 1 Tim.

4:1, 2); 50:4; Mark 14:38; John 3:8, 29; 5:19, 30; 8:42, 43, 47; 10; 18:37; 1 Corinthians 2:9, 10; Ephesians 6:18; 1 John 4:6, 13; etc.

In Scripture, the benefit of waiting in prayer is an opening of the heart to assurances from God that help and guidance are on the way. See Psalm 25:3, 5, 21; 27:14; 33:20; 37:7, 9; 38:15; 59:9; 62:1; Isaiah 38:18; 40:31; 49:23; Jeremiah 14:22; Lamentations 3:25, 26; Hosea 12:6; Micah 7:7; Zephaniah 3:8; Luke 12:3; etc.

> …blessed are all they that wait for him…And thine ears shall hear a word behind thee, saying, This is the way, walk ye in it, when ye turn to the right hand, and when ye turn to the left…. Then shall he give the rain of thy seed, that thou shalt sow the ground withal; and bread of the increase of the earth, and it shall be fat and plenteous: (Isaiah 30:18–23)

> We must individually hear Him speaking to the heart. When every other voice is hushed, and in quietness we wait before Him, the silence of the soul makes more distinct the voice of God. He bids us, "Be still, and know that I am God." Psalm 46:10. This is the effectual preparation for all labor for God. (White, *The Ministry of Healing*, p. 58)

> There are three ways in which the Lord reveals His will to us, to guide us, and to fit us to guide others. How may we know His voice from that of a stranger?? How shall we distinguish it from the voice of a false shepherd? God reveals His will to us in His word, the Holy Scriptures. His voice is also revealed in His providential workings; and it will be recognized if we do not separate our souls from Him by walking in our own ways… until the senses have become so confused that eternal things are not discerned, and the voice of Satan is so disguised that it is accepted as the voice of God.

> Another way in which God's voice is heard is through the appeals of His Holy Spirit, making impressions upon the heart, which will be wrought out in the character. (White, *Testimonies for the Church*, vol. 5, p. 512)

The treasures that tune the heart to God's voice are the keeping of appointed times set aside for Him—mornings, evenings, and the twenty-four-hour Sabbath day. May nothing being allowed to rob us of these small rain appointments.

The following is a list of Spirit of Prophecy references with brief summaries of their themes that will hopefully serve as a further resource for the study of abiding/communion:

> MH 85—He desires you to walk with Him in constant communion.
>
> 5T 651–654—Keep before you a sense of the constant presence of God.
>
> 5T 628—The necessity of the ever abiding sense of God's presence; power for moral and religious restraint.
>
> 5T 147—Do everything as if in the immediate presence of God.
>
> 1SM 114—Brought into hard and difficult places…cherish the abiding sense of God's power.
>
> TMK 193—"The longing desire for communion with God soon ceases when the Spirit of God is grieved from us, but when Christ is in us the hope of glory, we are constantly directed to think and act in reference to the glory of God."
>
> 2T 545—Faithful watchman listens for the Divine Teacher (see Luke 12:42); feed the flock in due season.
>
> EW 73—Letting go of the hand of the Lord too soon.
>
> 6T 64—Church body needs fresh and living experience of its members in habitual communion with God.

7BC 953—Divine intuition.

MH 509—Jesus' nights of prayer: before ordination of disciples, sermon on the mount, the transfiguration, agony of judgment hall and the cross, and the resurrection glory.

5T 221—Experimental religion needed now; taste and see that the Lord is good.

2T 230, 549—Watch, hear, and listen for Him

TM 508—No place to settle into a careless attitude; watch and pray; connection every moment essential.

8T 329—Enoch's experience.

8T 331—Experience of John the Baptist.

5T 224—John the Baptist, the greatest of prophets: "The friend of the bridegroom, which standeth and heareth him, rejoiceth greatly because of the bridegroom's voice: this my joy therefore is fulfilled."

MB 40—If we have no light, it is because we have no connection with the Source.

SD 360—Christ's followers lived in close contact; in constant communion with God; "They are prepared for the communion of heaven; for they have heaven in their hearts."

SC 87—God speaks to us through providence, His Spirit on the heart, and His Word.

MB 103—Prayer; the disciples had come to connect His hours of prayer with the power of His words and works.

MB 112—He seeks to draw us into communion through prayer and the study of His Word.

Perhaps God's voice is more familiar than we realize. Peter must have given some thought about the true identity of Jesus. Outspoken as he was, his answer came without hesitation. "...Thou art the Christ, the Son of the living God" (John 16;16). Nothing in the record indicates that Peter knew his words were inspired but Jesus, with a clear tone of joy, made known to

His hearers the true source of Peter's utterance. "Blessed art thou, Simon Bar-jona: for flesh and blood hath not revealed it unto thee, but my Father which is in heaven" (John 16:17). (See also John 10:4, 5, 16, 27, 28.) Here is one of if not the greatest attainments of the Christian life—an on-going availability for divine/human interaction placed above every other consideration. The seasons of waiting upon God are the golden opportunities that give a higher sense of purpose for our day. When that final day comes and we hear His trumpet voice, we will recognize it as that quiet voice we heard when communing with Him in this life. "Verily, verily, I say unto you, The hour is coming, and now is, when the dead shall hear the voice of the Son of God: and they that hear shall live" (John 5:25).

"Now we have received, not the spirit of the world, but the spirit which is of God; that we might know the things that are freely given to us of God" (1 Cor. 2:12). What is the significance of seeking to know these things? It means that spiritual things will become as much a reality as our physical world is along with an added benefit—living the Christian life will become natural.

> Love to God must be a living principle, underlying every act and word and thought. If in the strength of Christ we are seeking to maintain such a consecration, we shall be daily holding communion with God....The principles of God's law will dwell in the heart, and control the actions. It will then be as natural for us to seek purity and holiness, to shun the spirit and example of the world, and to seek to benefit all around us, as it is for the angels of glory to execute the mission of love assigned them. (White, *Sons and Daughters of God*, p. 51)

When we bring our lives to complete obedience to the law of God, regarding God as our supreme Guide, and clinging to Christ as our hope of righteousness, God will work in our behalf. This is a righteousness of faith....The commandments of God diligently studied and practiced, open to us communication with heaven, and distinguish for us the true from the false. This obedience works out for us the divine will, bringing into our lives the righteousness and perfection that was seen in the life of Christ. (White, *Sons and Daughters of God*, p. 66)

Monks from various religions devote years of their lives to master hearing God's voice while hidden away in remote monasteries and temples. However, finding daily fellowship with God has a practical outcome, especially when facing heightened opposition from demonic armies. "Communion with God imparts to the soul an intimate knowledge of His will" (White 1881, p. 534). There is much contentment and joy when, through communion with God, souls come to understand their divine purpose and the power which accompanies living out that purpose.

> *There is much contentment and joy when, through communion with God, souls come to understand their divine purpose and the power which accompanies living out that purpose.*

We have every evidence that Jesus is waiting to bless us. It is not his will that we should go forth to labor in his cause, and yet have no special help, no power from on high, to attend our labors. God has never bidden us hold up the standard of his law in these days of general apostasy, without the aid of divine power. We may have help from heaven, and we should not feel free to go to battle without the evidence that God's presence will attend us. (White, *Gospel Workers*, p. 460)

Listening to His voice results in greater progress and supplies courage to overcome barriers.

If they will listen to His voice and follow in His ways, God will correct and enlighten them, and bring them back to their upright position of distinction from the world. When the advantage of working upon Christian principles is discerned, when self is hid in Christ, much greater progress will be made; for each worker will feel his own human weakness; he will supplicate for the wisdom and grace of God, and will receive the divine help that is pledged for every emergency.

Opposing circumstances should create a firm determination to overcome them. One barrier broken down will give greater ability and courage to go forward. (White, *Testimonies for the Church*, vol. 6, p. 145)

The Greatest Work

"Now to him that worketh is the reward not reckoned of grace, but of debt. But to him that worketh not, but believeth on him that justifieth the ungodly, his faith is counted for righteousness" (Rom. 4:4, 5).

And yet how many are making laborious work of walking in the narrow way of holiness. To many the peace and rest of this blessed way seems no nearer today than it did years in the past. They look afar off for that which is nigh; they make intricate that which Jesus made very plain. He is "the way, the truth, and the life." The plan of salvation has been plainly revealed in the word of God; but the wisdom of the world has been sought too much, and the wisdom of Christ's righteousness too little. And souls that might have rested in the love of Jesus, have been doubting, and troubled about many things. (White, *The Review and Herald*, July 1, 1884, par. 2)

While home on furlough from church planting with Adventist Frontier Missions, Brian and Duang Wilson decided to help their local church with construction. Brian wrote, "I joined the team of volunteers and was assigned the task of drilling holes in the foundation of the building in preparation for a sidewalk. In spite of my good intentions, I found drilling through cement an impossible task. I strained every muscle until large beads of sweat dripped from my forehead. I knelt, sat, and leaned in various ways hoping for an optimal position from which to drill. I measured my progress in nanometers.

"Finally, in desperation, *I asked the man in charge* what I was doing wrong. He looked at the drill and said it wasn't adjusted properly. There was a hammer function for drilling through cement. After making the adjustment, I drilled the holes with ease. I had been trying to drill through the cement on my own strength. But when I set it properly, the drill did all the work for me. All I had to do was hold it and push a little" ("No Title," *Adventist Frontiers*, January, 2005, emphasis added).

"Then said they unto him, What shall we do, that we might work the works of God? Jesus answered and said unto them, This is the work of God, that ye believe on him whom he hath sent" (John 6:28, 29). Also, "…greater works than these shall he [the Holy Spirit] do…" (John 14:12). The early/small rains and abiding in Christ are one and the same. This is the yoke which Jesus says makes it a light burden to serve Him (see Matt. 11:28).

> As God's people, we have a special work to do. All who have submitted their will to the will of God are to become laborers together with him. The invitation of Christ is: "Come unto me, all ye that labor and are heavy laden, and I will give you rest. Take *my yoke* upon you, and learn of me; for I am meek and lowly in heart: and ye shall find rest unto your souls. For my yoke is easy, and my burden is light." (White, *The Review and Herald*, November 29, 1898, par. 1)

"The moment His yoke is adjusted to your neck, that moment it is found easy; then the heaviest spiritual labor can be performed, the heaviest burdens borne, because the Lord gives the strength and the power, and he gives gladness in doing the work. Mark the points: 'Learn of me; for I am meek and lowly in heart' (Matthew 11:29). Who is it that speaks thus?—The Majesty of heaven, the King of glory. He desires that your conception of spiritual things shall be purified from the dross of selfishness, the defilement of a crooked, coarse, unsympathetic nature. You must have an inward, higher experience. You must obtain a growth in grace by abiding in Christ. When you are converted, you will not be a hindrance, but will strengthen your brethren."

As these words were spoken, I saw that some turned sadly away and mingled with the scoffers. Others, with tears, all broken in heart, made confession to those whom they had bruised and wounded. They did not think of maintaining their own dignity, but asked at every step. "What must I do to be saved?" (Acts 16:30). The answer was, "Repent, and be converted, that your sins may go beforehand to judgment, and be blotted out." (White, *Selected Messages*, book 1, pp. 110–111)

Human nature is ever struggling for expression. He who is made complete in Christ must first be emptied of pride, of self-sufficiency. Then there is silence in the soul, and God's voice can be heard. Then the Spirit can find unobstructed entrance. Let God work in and through you. (White, *The Signs of the Times*, April 9, 1902, par. 12)

And Moses said unto the people, Fear ye not, stand still, and see the salvation of the LORD, which he will shew to you to day: for the Egyptians [your slave masters, obstacles of the world contending against our faith] whom ye have seen to day, ye shall see them again no more for ever. The LORD shall fight for you, and ye shall hold your peace. (Exodus 14:13–14)

The word "communion" is represented by the burning of the lamps fed by the oil of God's Spirit that keeps the five wise virgins connected and ready until the midnight cry of Jesus at the door's threshold. They enter for the seal of God and harvest ripening rain. Then the communion of their burning lamps will be a light globally visible through the power of the Revelation 18 angel, who joins the third angel in the message to be given to earth.

God will use ways and means by which it will be seen that He is taking the reins in His own hands. The workers will be surprised by the simple means that He will use to bring about and perfect His work of righteousness. Those who are accounted good workers will need to draw nigh to God, they will need the divine touch. They will need to drink more deeply and continuously at the fountain of living water, in order that they may discern God's work at every point. (White, *Testimonies to Ministers and Gospel Workers*, p. 300)

Christ Comes to the Soul's Door and Heaven's Temple Door

When people enjoy nature, they sense a certain ownership of their space, where there are no walls and the ceiling is the sky; but when entering a door, they immediately recognize either their own domain or someone else's. The allegory of entering with Christ into the wedding/supper hall alludes to becoming household members in the domain of communion with the Father and Son.

There are key words in common with all the wedding parables—chiefly, the banquet hall and door through which the bridegroom and guests enter for the honor of joining the great supper. All of these represent the judgment in progress that is soon closing because the guests, having gone through admission and inspection, are now being served from the king's table, which encompasses not only physical food, but also "every word that proceedeth out of the mouth of God."

When Matthew 25:6 says "the bridegroom cometh," it is certainly fitting to think of His visible coming in the general sense. However, specifically, it is His coming to the saints via the Holy Spirit to have a spiritual supper with them through communion-level faith, prior to His visible coming. This is revealed by the second wedding parable of Luke 14:12–25 above and Luke 12:35–46 below.

Luke 12 continues the wedding theme and includes the same scene of Jesus as is found in Revelation 3:19–20, with His appeal to the seventh church when He comes knocking at our souls' door. Those found wearing the wedding garment furnished for them open the door without fear, and thus they are set for the next shadow-fulfillment festival, shortly to begin in the next section.

The Soul's Door

> Let your loins be girded about [with the proper garment, i.e. white robe], and your lights burning; And ye yourselves like unto men that wait for their lord, when he will return from the wedding; that when he cometh and knocketh, they may open unto him immediately. Blessed are those servants, whom the lord when he cometh shall find watching: verily I say unto you, that he shall gird himself, and make them to sit down to meat, and will come forth and serve them. And if he shall come in the second watch, or come in the third watch, and find them

so, blessed are those servants. And this know, that if the goodman of the house had known what hour the thief would come, he would have watched, and not have suffered his house to be broken through. Be ye therefore ready also: for the Son of man cometh at an hour when ye think not. Then Peter said unto him, Lord, speakest thou this parable unto us, or even to all? And the Lord said, Who then is that faithful and wise steward, whom his lord shall make ruler over his household, to give them their portion of meat in due season? Blessed is that servant, whom his lord when he cometh shall find so doing. Of a truth I say unto you, that he will make him ruler over all that he hath. But and if that servant say in his heart, My lord delayeth his coming; and shall begin to beat the menservants and maidens, and to eat and drink, and to be drunken; The lord of that servant will come in a day when he looketh not for him, and at an hour when he is not aware, and will cut him in sunder, and will appoint him his portion with the unbelievers. (Luke 12:35–46)

Because of the fact that He knocks, could the coming of Luke 12:36 be the second advent? Could this represent the visible, earth-shaking coming of Christ, or something else? Will Jesus "knock" on the world before the skies are rolled back? The answer, in part, is another question—have there been misunderstandings about His coming before?

When this is limited to represent only the second advent, then that special coming of Christ *via the Holy Spirit* may be overlooked. Jesus promised this manner of His coming as follows: "And I will pray the Father, and He shall give you another Comforter, that he may abide with you for ever; even the Spirit of truth; whom the world cannot receive, because it seeth him not, neither knoweth him: but ye know him; for he dwelleth with you, and shall be in you. I will not leave you comfortless: I will come to you" (John 14:16–18).

Thus, here is a coming of Christ through the Holy Spirit. Yes, this has been available since the creation of mankind, but not to the same extent globally. The power and teachings of the Holy Spirit, for most centuries of fallen humanity, are represented as dew and small rains, so that believers might avail themselves with spiritual preparations (extra oil for the lamps) for the seasons of the greater rain later. Pentecost and Tabernacles are the occasions for unrestrained visitations of Christ through the Holy Spirit.

The two key words in Luke 12:36–37 are "wait" and "watching." They also appear in Proverbs 8:34–35: "Blessed is the man that heareth me, watching daily at my gates, waiting at the posts of my doors. For whoso findeth me findeth life, and shall obtain favour of the LORD."

What door/gate is this in Luke 12 and Proverbs 8? "He is only waiting to be invited by us with earnest heart, with sincere desire. Nothing is wanting but a preparation of heart, and earnest, believing prayer, to bring Jesus to our side as a mighty helper. He longs to come. If we will but listen to his voice and open the door, he will come in" (White 1892, p. 225).

This wedding door (of the soul) opening today is the availability of constant replenishment by daily communing with God, especially at the start of the day, symbolized by the manna which was to be gathered before it melted under the heat of the sun (see Exod. 16:21).

"Prepare the heart for the reception of the Holy Spirit, that it may have free course in the entire being. Open the door of the soul-temple, and let the Saviour in. 'Behold, I stand at the door, and knock,' he says. 'If any man hear my voice, and open the door, I will come in to him, and will sup with him, and he with me'" (White, December 13, 1906, par. 18).

Heaven's Temple Door

The seed-germinating parable of Mark 4 reminds us that when the fruit (during the latter rain) is brought forth, He *immediately* puts forth the sickle. This is a coming to the door of the sanctuary when He meets His people at midnight, a chapter of history when earth reaches its lowest point. In Revelation, this door first appears with the sixth church of Philadelphia, which in history represents the birth of Adventism and the Day of Atonement shadow fulfillment message (see Rev. 3:7, 8; 14:6–8).

Christ has entered the door of heaven's atoning judgment, which now being open cannot be shut, preparing a congregation for reflecting His righteousness. It remains open until this condition is met. Then the Bridegroom stands at the door to close it because His high-priestly ministry is soon to cease. "The signs which He Himself gave of His coming have been fulfilled, and by the teaching of God's word we may know that the Lord is at the door" (White 1900, p. 227).

This coming is a silent one, just as the coming of Christ to the Ancient of Days in 1844 was. However, it will be clear to the saints from the developments taking place afterward that the coming of the Holy Spirit has occurred. Outward evidences that follow this coming are covered in chapter 8.

"And the glory of the God of Israel was gone up from the cherub, whereupon he was, to the threshold of the house. And he called to the man clothed with linen, which had the writer's inkhorn by his side" (Ezek. 9:3). Ezekiel 8 portrays doors where abominations among God's people are seen; nothing is hidden. "And the LORD said unto him, Go through the midst of the city, through the midst of Jerusalem, and set a mark upon the foreheads of the men that sigh and that cry for all the abominations that be done in the midst thereof" (9:4).

That mark, as further study reveals, is the mark of the new covenant—God's laws written upon the tables of the heart, especially Sabbath rest (see Ezek. 20:12, 20; Eph. 4:24–31), the sacred 24-hour divine appointment—ample opportunity for gathering oil.

> "And to the others he said in mine hearing, Go ye after him through the city, and smite: let not your eye spare, neither have ye pity: Slay utterly old and young, both maids, and little

children, and women: but come not near any man upon whom is the mark; and begin at my sanctuary. Then they began at the ancient men which were before the house." (Ezekiel 9:5–6)

Every case had been decided for life or death. While Jesus had been ministering in the sanctuary, the judgment had been going on for the righteous dead, and then for the righteous living. Christ had received His kingdom, having made the atonement for His people and blotted out their sins. <u>The subjects of the kingdom were made up</u>. The marriage of the Lamb was consummated. And the kingdom, and the greatness of the kingdom under the whole heaven, was given to Jesus and the heirs of salvation, and Jesus was to reign as King of kings and Lord of lords. (White, *Early Writings*, p. 280)

With such a future just before us, how do the Scriptures express God's urgent appeal?

"If therefore thou shalt not watch, I will come on thee as a thief, and thou shalt not know what hour I will come upon thee" (Rev. 3:3).

"Jesus has left us word: 'Watch ye therefore: for ye know not when the Master of the house cometh, at even, or at midnight, or at the cockcrowing, or in the morning: lest coming suddenly He find you sleeping. And what I say unto you I say unto all, Watch'" (White 1871, p. 190; see also Matt. 25:5–6 and Mark 13:35–36).

To watch and pray is a fairly light burden for something so powerful—continued replenishment of the oil for our lamps and a defense against daily attacks from the fallen angels. White continues:

We are waiting and watching for the return of the Master, who is to bring the morning, lest coming suddenly He find us sleeping. What time is here referred to? Not to the revelation of Christ in the clouds of heaven to find a people asleep.

No; but to His return from His ministration in the most holy place of the heavenly sanctuary, when He lays off His priestly attire and clothes Himself with garments of vengeance, and when the mandate goes forth: "He that is unjust, let him be unjust still: and he which is filthy, let him be filthy still: and he that is righteous, let him be righteous still; and he that is holy, let him be holy still. (*Testimonies for the Church*, vol. 2, p. 190–191).

Mark 13:35–36, quoted above, again confirms a judgment ending that comes silently, without earthly signs or wonders. This is due to the fact that the ending point for the judgment is based upon what has been taking place entirely in heaven—examination of our books of records, the pages of which have been filled with the writings of the holy angels. "Having received the kingdom, He will come in His glory, as King of kings and Lord of lords, for the redemption of His people, who are to 'sit down with Abraham, and Isaac, and Jacob' at His table in His kingdom, to partake of the marriage supper of the Lamb" (White 1952, p. 356). This is a literal marriage supper around God's throne, yet clearly there is a figurative supper promised to the last church—communion with God through the bread of the Word for the remnant to carry out their last mission (see Rev. 3:20; refer to the next chapter).

James associates this scene of the Lord standing at the door with the closing judgment and outpouring of rain revival:

> Be patient therefore, brethren, unto the coming of the Lord. Behold, the husbandman waiteth for the precious fruit of the earth, and hath long patience for it, until he receive the early and latter rain. Be ye also patient; stablish your hearts: for the coming of the Lord draweth nigh. Grudge not one against another, brethren, lest ye be condemned: behold, the judge standeth before the door. (James 5:7–9)

It's not a problem to apply "the coming of the Lord" to the visible return of Jesus, but in consideration of the previous related passages, James is writing of the coming of Christ via the Holy Spirit to prepare for the closing judgment, as well as the Spirit's outpouring rain to nourish the soul with the supper of present truth, making straight the path of the Lord.

Chapter 4

The Feast of Tabernacles Shadow Fulfillment

Once Christlike character is our character, God will be pleased to send His final release of divine power—the global outpouring of the Holy Spirit. This last global visitation is of such unprecedented vitality that He is able to elevate earth from its continuing descent into spiritual gloom up to the last step of heaven's stairway. This is the breakthrough for the last conditions, starting with the often-cited words of Jesus: "And this gospel of the kingdom shall be preached in all the world for a witness unto all nations; and then shall the end come" (Matt. 24:14).

> *Once Christlike character is our character, God will be pleased to send His final release of divine power—the global outpouring of the Holy Spirit.*

In conjunction with covering the globe with the everlasting gospel is the achievement of the fourth goal—God's house being filled with souls gathered from the "highways and hedges" (Luke 14:23) and fully restored. It may be said that as a result of the combination of church tasks and divine power, the Lord's one great objective will be accomplished—a multitude of living saints to greet Him when He comes, as opposed to merely a handful that survived earth's first destruction by water.

This living multitude will be many more than 144,000 individuals. Consider that the Bible manner of counting populations is by heads of households: "The number of those who ate was four thousand men, besides women and children" (Matt. 15:38, NIV; see also Num. 1:1–4 and Gal. 6:10). After hearing the number 144,000, John turns his head and sees a multitude which cannot be numbered (see Rev. 7:9).

Although the condition of carrying the gospel to the world has been the main mission of the church until now, Satan's opposition has made it such that this barrier remains elusive until that day when God's outpouring manifestation takes us across the barrier to the finish line. All of this awaits the door—the church's character goal—yet to be fully opened. No one is suggesting that carrying forth the gospel should be suspended until the character goal is reached. Sharing the gospel is essential for character formation, but neglect of character will assure that the Matthew 24:14 barrier remains insurmountable due to the lack of divine power, and it won't matter how much technology and resources are in place.

	Annual Feast Type	Outcome
5.	**Day of Tabernacles** (Booths): **Latter Rain** ("2nd Pentecost"), **Sealing**, and **Return of Christ** for harvest Reaping. (Zech. 14)	Final release of Divine power, then 3rd and 4th Remnant Church tasks, finishing the gospel and filling God's house

> Speak unto the children of Israel, saying, The fifteenth day of this seventh month shall be the feast of tabernacles for seven days unto the LORD. On the first day shall be an holy convocation: ye shall do no servile work therein. Seven days ye shall offer an offering made by fire unto the LORD: on the eighth day shall be an holy convocation unto you; and ye shall offer an

offering made by fire unto the LORD: it is a solemn assembly; and ye shall do no servile work therein. These are the feasts of the LORD, which ye shall proclaim to be holy convocations, to offer an offering made by fire unto the LORD, a burnt offering, and a meat offering, a sacrifice, and drink offerings, every thing upon his day: Beside the sabbaths of the LORD, and beside your gifts, and beside all your vows, and beside all your freewill offerings, which ye give unto the LORD. Also in the fifteenth day of the seventh month, when ye have gathered in the fruit of the land, ye shall keep a feast unto the LORD seven days: on the first day shall be a sabbath, and on the eighth day shall be a sabbath. And ye shall take you on the first day the boughs of goodly trees, branches of palm trees, and the boughs of thick trees, and willows of the brook; and ye shall rejoice before the LORD your God seven days. (Leviticus 23:34–40)

Recall that the yearly holy feasts represent the shadow fulfillments of the dispensation of the entire Christian age—phases of Christ's ministry since becoming our High Priest until now (see Col. 2:16, 17). "They do not say in their heart, 'Let us now fear the Lord our God, who gives rain, both the former and the latter, in its season. He reserves for us the appointed weeks of the harvest'" (Jer. 5:24, NKJV). The Feast of Tabernacles is the last annual shadow fulfillment and represents the final movements of the global harvest gathering, ending with the wilderness hiding places where His children will have retreated right before His appearing. Prophetically, Tabernacles is often referred to as the second Pentecost. In preparation for Tabernacles, the saints have the daily Elijah-type, communion level of righteousness which they each build around themselves—a personal faith tabernacle with the Lord that persists in a world of steadily diminishing godliness and love (see Matt. 24:12). "For in the time of trouble he shall hide me in his pavilion: in the secret of his tabernacle shall he hide me; he shall set me up upon a rock" (Ps. 27:5).

Ancient Israel celebrated Tabernacles just five days after the Day of Atonement, when their hearts were still deeply affected by the solemn guilt-atoning activities of the high priest entering the Holy of holies. Tabernacles was comprised of holy days of rejoicing, when the people were no longer under the burden of past sins and even freed from the burdens of household and workplace duties. They enjoyed days in the outdoors under the bows and branches of nearby trees and shrubs. The measure of renewal and peace of mind during Tabernacles was a result of faithful participation in the cleansing of the Day of Atonement. Those who did not afflict themselves with soul-searching, confession, and repentance disqualified themselves, or in the words of Moses, were "cut off" from the blessings of Tabernacles. As for the congregation at large, they were cleansed during Atonement and thus prepared for Tabernacles, the holiday of rejoicing while dwelling in their booths of green foliage, a type of heaven on earth.

In the closing moments of the Day of Atonement, the names of the remnant saints appointed for the seal of the Father are retained in the Lamb's book of life (see Rev. 7). During that time is sounded the midnight cry of Matthew 25 when they enter the wedding supper for final movement guidance and the door is closed to the unsealed of the flock. The entering of this door represents going up to spiritual Jerusalem for the feast of Tabernacles (see Zech. 14:16–21; Heb. 12:22–27). The scattered sheep not of this fold and still in Babylon are the next to be sealed as they receive the call of God given by the wise virgins under the power of the latter rain showering down at the same time. Then His scattered are gathered into one sealed flock (see John 10) and prepared for the global close of probation and second coming shortly after. The success accompanying the culminating Feast of Tabernacles assures that His coming is quickened, and in such a manner as to fill God's house with abundance.

"It [the coming of the Lord] will not tarry past the time that the message is borne to all nations, tongues, and peoples. Shall we who claim to be students of prophecy forget that God's forbearance to the wicked is a part of the vast and merciful plan by which He is seeking to compass the salvation of souls" (White 1946, p. 697)?

As shown further, there are three inspired passages designating Tabernacles as the feast when the latter rain begins. The third one near the end of this section is in the form of a prayer offered by King Solomon. How important are the early rain and dews with respect to having a part in the latter rain of Tabernacles?

> Many have in a great measure failed to receive the former rain. They have not obtained all the benefits that God has thus provided for them. They expect that the lack will be supplied by the latter rain. When the richest abundance of grace shall be bestowed, they intend to open their hearts to receive it. They are making a terrible mistake. The work that God has begun in the human heart in giving His light and knowledge must be continually going forward. Every individual must realize his own necessity. The heart must be emptied of every defilement and cleansed for the indwelling of the Spirit. *It was by the confession and forsaking of sin, by earnest prayer and consecration of themselves to God, that the early disciples prepared for the outpouring of the Holy Spirit on the Day of Pentecost.* The same work, only in greater degree, must be done now. Then the human agent had only to ask for the blessing, and wait for the Lord to perfect the work concerning him. It is God who began the work, and He will finish His work, making man complete in Jesus Christ. But there must be no neglect of the grace represented by the former rain. Only those who are living up to the light they have will receive greater light. Unless we are daily advancing in the exemplification of the active Christian virtues, we shall not recognize the manifestations of the Holy Spirit in the latter rain. It may be falling on hearts all around us, but we shall not discern or receive it.

At no point in our experience can we dispense with the assistance of that which enables us to make the first start. The blessings received under the former rain are needful to us to the end. Yet these alone will not suffice. While we cherish the blessing of the early rain, we must not, on the other hand, lose sight of the fact that without the latter rain, to fill out the ears and ripen the grain, the harvest will not be ready for the sickle, and the labor of the sower will have been in vain. Divine grace is needed at the beginning, divine grace at every step of advance, and divine grace alone can complete the work. (White, *Testimonies to Ministers and Gospel Workers*, pp. 507–508, emphasis added)

The Lord calls for united action. Well organized efforts must be made to secure laborers. There are poor, honest, humble souls whom the Lord will put in your places, who have never had the opportunities you have had and could not because you were not worked by the Holy Spirit. We may be sure that when the Holy Spirit is poured out, those who did not receive and appreciate the early rain will not see or understand the value of the latter rain. When we are truly consecrated to God, His love will abide in our hearts by faith and we will cheerfully do our duty, in accordance with the will of God. (White, *Manuscript Releases*, vol. 1, p. 180)

Zechariah's Prophecy of the Latter Rain

And it shall come to pass, that every one that is left of all the nations which came against Jerusalem shall even go up from year to year to worship the King, the LORD of hosts, and to keep the feast of tabernacles. And it shall be, that whoso will not come up of all the families of the earth unto Jerusalem to worship the King, the LORD of hosts, even upon them shall be no rain. And if the family of Egypt go not up, and come not, that have no rain; there shall be the plague, wherewith the LORD will smite the heathen that come not up to keep the feast of tabernacles. This shall be the punishment of Egypt, and the punishment of all nations that come not up to keep the feast of tabernacles. (Zechariah 14:16–19)

Jesus promised the first outpouring of Pentecost in Luke 24 and Acts 1, but did He associate Tabernacles with the latter rain? In John 7, He does appear to at least allude to this, but it doesn't become apparent until verse 38, where on the last day of Tabernacles He speaks of "rivers of living water," which would come flowing down after heavy rain.

Now the Jews' feast of tabernacles was at hand. His brethren therefore said unto him, Depart hence, and go into Judaea, that thy disciples also may see the works that thou doest.... But when his brethren were gone up, then went he also up unto the feast, not openly, but as it were in secret [The future Tabernacles fulfillment begins, as it were, in secret, without any prior outward signs]. In the last day, that great day of the feast, Jesus stood and cried, saying, If any man thirst, let him come unto me, and drink. He that believeth on me, as the scripture hath said, out of his belly shall flow rivers of living water. (But this spake he of the Spirit, which they that believe on him should receive: for the Holy Ghost was not yet given; because that Jesus was not yet glorified.) (John 7:2, 3, 10, 37–39)

This is true of both Pentecost and Tabernacles. They are parallel outpourings, one at the start and the other at the finish for carrying the gospel to the nations. Through divine visitation, the first provided coverage to the world of the Roman Empire, and the second, coverage to every nation and people of earth.

Global Scale of Rains Compared— The Work of a Single Generation

Many centuries before the remnant formed, Paul notes that as a result of the first Pentecost, the whole world heard the gospel. "But they have not all obeyed the gospel. For Esaias saith, Lord, who hath believed our report? So then faith cometh by hearing, and hearing by the word of God. But I say, Have they not heard? Yes verily, their sound went into *all the earth*, and their words unto the *ends of the world*" (Rom. 10:16–18, emphasis added; see also 16:25, 26).

"For the hope which is laid up for you in heaven, whereof ye heard before in the word of the truth of the gospel; Which is come unto you, as it is in all the world; and bringeth forth fruit, as it doth also in you, since the day ye heard of it, and knew the grace of God in truth" (Col. 1:5, 6).

"First, I thank my God through Jesus Christ for you all, that your faith is spoken of *throughout the whole world*" (Rom. 1:8, emphasis added).

Was the preaching of the gospel and last message to all tribes finished during the first century? Was it a contradiction for Peter to apply the promise "I will pour out my Spirit upon all flesh" in describing the Pentecost of His day? Actually, it is a parallel/dual fulfillment, the first of which we might say was a smaller-scale precursor. The early rain of Pentecost accomplished the same success for the known world of the first century as the latter rain will for the entire earth (Revelation 18:1 is very specific about this promise, as will be seen later). This parallel emphasis on the whole world should not be overlooked. As with the first, so with the second outpouring, once it commences, the generation who receives it is assured of seeing their world covered with the gospel.

> The work of the disciples was to spread a knowledge of the gospel. To them was committed the work of proclaiming to all the world the good news that Christ brought to men. *That work they accomplished for the people of their time. To every nation under*

heaven the gospel was carried in a single generation. (White, *The Ministry of Healing*, p. 141, emphasis added)

Then was there such a revelation of the glory of Christ as had never before been witnessed by mortal man. Multitudes who had reviled His name and despised His power confessed themselves disciples of the Crucified. Through the cooperation of the divine Spirit the labors of the humble men whom Christ had chosen stirred the world. To every nation under heaven was the gospel carried *in a single generation*. (White, *The Publishing Ministry*, p. 270, emphasis added)

Prior to opening the gates for heaven's showers on Pentecost, what determined that the time was right? Something happened among the disciples gathered in the upper room that brought them into a spiritual nature favorable for power from on high. It was as simple as a church fully clothed in Christ's likeness through a time set apart for continual prayer, repentance, and confession. Within a few days, not years, they received the promised outpouring. Due to today's urgency, there may be expected the same rapid response under the very same conditions, on a global scale.

> *Prior to opening the gates for heaven's showers on Pentecost, what determined that the time was right? Something happened among the disciples gathered in the upper room that brought them into a spiritual nature favorable for power from on high.*

"Would it not be well for you to seek the Lord as the disciples sought Him before the day of Pentecost? After

Christ's ascension, His disciples—men of varied talents and capabilities—assembled in an upper chamber to pray for the gift of the Holy Spirit. In this room 'all continued with one accord in prayer and supplication.' They made thorough work of repentance by confessing their own sins. Upon them was laid no burden to confess one another's sins. Settling all differences and alienations, they were of one accord, and prayed with unity of purpose for ten days, at the end of which time 'they were all filled with the Holy Ghost, and began to speak with other tongues, as the Spirit gave them utterance.' (White, *Manuscript Releases*, vol. 7, pp. 94–95)

This extraordinary cooperation with the Holy Spirit is an exact comparison with the second outpouring. The one exception is the area of coverage. In our time, the unfulfilled prophecies of Joel 2 will be completed as such: "I will pour out My Spirit on all flesh;" that is, from pole to pole. In the language of Revelation 14:6 and 10:11, it will be "every nation, and kindred, and tongue, and people."

In the case of the second outpouring, that generation is assured of being the last one to have inhabited fallen earth, the one that will welcome Jesus to earth after having gone through the time of trouble (see Ps. 91) when God's wrath is poured out upon the impenitent for a short time. "At that time the 'latter rain,' or refreshing from the presence of the Lord, will come, to give power to the loud voice of the third angel, and prepare the saints to stand in the period when the seven last plagues shall be poured out" (White 1882, p. 86).

"And the sixth angel poured out his vial upon the great river Euphrates; and the water thereof was dried up, that the way of the kings of the east might be prepared" (Rev. 16:12).

At the instant of the last outpouring, the words of Jesus can be fully applied: "Verily I say unto you, This generation shall not pass away, till all be fulfilled" (Luke 21:32).

The previous verse comes from Jesus' discourse on both the end of Jerusalem and the end of the world as a dualistic prophecy. From the context, it was spoken to the apostles as applying to their day, but historically, some of the chapter reveals the future far beyond the apostles, namely the times of the Gentiles. "And there shall be signs in the sun, and in the moon, and in the stars; and upon the earth distress of nations, with perplexity; the sea and the waves roaring" (v. 25; consider the tsunamis of 2004 and 2011). The present generation is the one for which all these prophecies have now become past history, making available to it the promise that they will not pass away "till all be fulfilled."

> The dispensation in which we are now living is to be, to those that ask, the dispensation of the Holy Spirit. Ask for His blessing. It is time we were more intense in our devotion. To us is committed the arduous, but happy, glorious work of revealing Christ to those who are in darkness. We are called to proclaim the special truths for this time. For all this the outpouring of the Spirit is essential. We should pray for it. The Lord expects us to ask Him. We have not been wholehearted in this work....
>
> ...What we need is the quickening influence of the Holy Spirit of God. "Not by might, nor by power, but by My Spirit, saith the Lord of hosts." Pray without ceasing, and watch by working in accordance with your prayers. As you pray, believe, trust in God. *It is the time of the latter rain, when the Lord will give largely of His Spirit.* Be fervent in prayer, and watch in the Spirit. (White, *Testimonies to Ministers and Gospel Workers*, p. 511–512, emphasis added)

Only through this extra power is there any possibility of moving forward the day of the Lord, since Satan has had so much of a foothold in this world since the beginning of sin. In order to break his hold on the masses, God's outpouring prevails. There is no need to ponder 'How long?' until the outpouring, since we know that rather than time-based fulfillment, it is condition-based fulfillment. May this help us to set aside the disposition to let Christ come when He wants to come.

> We cannot exert a correct influence when we are under a cloud of anxiety and depression. We must reach out the hand of faith, and grasp the hand of our Redeemer. We must not wait for the latter rain. It is coming upon all who will recognize and appropriate the dew and showers of grace that fall upon us. When we gather up the fragments of light, when we appreciate the sure mercies of God, who loves to have us trust Him, then every promise will be fulfilled. "For as the earth bringeth forth her bud, and as the garden causeth the things that are sown in it to spring forth; so the Lord God will cause righteousness and praise to spring forth before all the nations" (Isaiah 61:11). (White, *Manuscript Releases*, vol. 1, pp. 177–178)

This is quite an eye-opening quotation because it indicates that the mission-finishing turning point is and has been held out before us for the taking for some time. As it says, "We must not wait for the latter rain." This tells me that the latter rain depends not on how God sees earth's state of affairs, but upon our collective desire to walk the path to the rain. A lingering question is, How many lesser preoccupations are holding things up from unbridled, global, spiritual power? Also, are we believing and sharing the second advent, but actually hesitant about daring to think the last outpouring could potentially arrive in our time?

Earlier it was noted that the preferred signs for which to watch were those within the church. If the primary signs for which the saints are watching are Sunday laws, they will literally come later rather than sooner, similar to the latter rain. Any diversion from following the signposts on God's roadmap is a cause of delay. In the meantime, Satan's greater goal is reached—we remain lukewarm, and for that reason, the need for Sunday laws diminishes. Like any war strategist, he knows that using a final solution too soon would only encourage the church to run to Jesus, the last thing he wants to see. The Sunday crisis only rises as a last counterattack when Satan sees evidence of God's power breaking forth. The latter rain is poured out because the church's conditions are coming to fruition and they can be trusted with unrestricted power. Shortly after this, the voice of God will be heard saying, "It is done" (Rev. 16:17; see chapter 8 of this volume). "The descent of the Holy Spirit upon the church is looked forward to as in the future; but <u>it is the privilege of the church to have it now</u>. Seek for it, pray for it, believe for it. We must have it, and Heaven is waiting to bestow it" (White 1946, p. 701).

> I have no specific time of which to speak when the outpouring of the Holy Spirit will take place…my message is that our only safety is in being ready for the heavenly refreshing, having our lamps trimmed and burning. Christ has told us to watch [hear, listen—2T 549]; "for in such an hour as ye think not, the Son of Man cometh." "Watch and pray" is the charge that is given us by our Redeemer.…Repent and be converted, that your sins may be blotted out when the times of refreshing <u>shall come</u> from the presence of the Lord. (White, *Selected Messages*, book 1, p. 192)

Both comings in that paragraph are the same event—the midnight coming of the heavenly refreshing to give both the rain and the latter seal of the Father (expanded shortly).

Wedding Continues with Reception Supper

In most cultures from antiquity, immediately after the wedding ceremony is when the real celebrating begins. Therefore, included with the wedding parables is the symbolic supper, an event of prophecy. This supper is supplied with food made possible by the rain of the Spirit. "I am the bread of life.... It is the Spirit who gives life; the flesh profits nothing. The words that I speak to you are spirit and *they* are life" (John 6:48, 63). "Again, he sent forth other servants, saying, Tell them which are bidden, Behold, I have prepared my dinner" (Matt. 22:4).

To the last generation church, Jesus says, "As many as I love, I rebuke and chasten: be zealous therefore, and repent. Behold, I stand at the door, and knock: if any man hear my voice, and open the door, I will come in to him, and will sup with him, and he with me" (Rev. 3:19, 20).

> And ye yourselves like unto men that wait for their lord, when he will return from the wedding; that when he cometh and knocketh, they may open unto him immediately. Blessed are those servants, whom the lord when he cometh shall find watching: verily I say unto you, that he shall gird himself, and make them to sit down to meat, and will come forth and serve them. (Luke 12:36–37).

That last verse contains one of the activities promised to us when we are served by Jesus after arriving in heaven. This certainly must be a literal promise, but we also find here a dual application that symbolically speaks of a spiritual meal prepared for us. Supping with Christ and He with us in the last days is a partaking in advancing Scripture light that guides us through the maze of final deceptions. We will know His voice from that of a stranger (see John 10).

How do the spiritual dews and small rain revivals succeed for the church in completing righteousness? For those who have accustomed themselves to communion with God during the early and maturing dew and small rains, God's voice will be readily discerned during the latter rain. Reiterating an earlier comment, soul-searching repentance is the door opener to the banquet hall of the remnant and the accompanying Elijah movement.

"Or despisest thou the riches of his goodness and forbearance and longsuffering; not knowing that the goodness of God leadeth thee to repentance" (Rom. 2:4)? Today, what happens when Laodicea opens the door of repentance and partakes in communion-level righteousness (see Rev. 3:20)? They go through the door to the supper when the midnight cry is given (see Matt. 25:6).

The Bible uses the metaphor of early dew and latter rain to represent the power accompanying His Word (bread), especially pertaining to the present time. The combination of fresh bread and power is the fuel of revival. Every genuine revival in history, such as the Reformation, Methodist movement, and Second Advent awakening, has been accompanied by new Scripture enlightenment and a restoration of former light.

> *Every genuine revival in history, such as the Reformation, Methodist movement, and Second Advent awakening, has been accompanied by new Scripture enlightenment and a restoration of former light.*

The first outpouring operated as an unrestrained convicting of the Holy Spirit based on new light—Jesus being the fulfillment of the Messianic prophecies—preached in the clearest and most convincing manner. Luke 12:42–43 ties in very well, particularly the last statement: "And the Lord said, Who then is that faithful and wise steward, whom his lord shall make ruler over his household, to give them their portion of meat in due season? Blessed is that servant, whom his lord when he cometh shall find so doing."

"For as rain comes down, and the snow from heaven, And do not return there, But water the earth, And make it bring forth and bud, That it may give seed to the sower and bread to the eater, So shall My word be that goes forth from My mouth; It shall not return to Me void, But it shall accomplish what I please" (Isa. 55:10, 11, NKJV). Here we have clear statements regarding bread representing the Word of God. This has and will have an integral part in the former and latter rain. The prophecy is that His Word shall (future) not return to Him void, but shall (future) accomplish what He purposes.

The remnant members, supping with Him (see Rev. 3:20), all recognize the same Word. The food of the marriage supper is the guiding words of Jesus falling as rain (Deut. 32:2; for example, through scattered small groups), with confirmation coming from the New Testament prophetic gift in their midst. "And he saith unto me, Write, Blessed are they which are called unto the marriage supper of the Lamb.... And I fell at his feet to worship him. And he said unto me, See thou do it not: I am thy fellowservant, and of thy brethren that have the testimony of Jesus: worship God: for the testimony of Jesus is the spirit of prophecy" (Rev. 19:9, 10).

> The influence of the work we are doing will be felt through all eternity. If we will work in harmony with one another and with heaven, God will demonstrate his power in our behalf as he did for the disciples on the day of Pentecost. Those days of preparation, in which the disciples prepared themselves by prayer and a putting away of all disunion, brought them into such close relation to God that he could work for them and through them in a marvelous manner. Today God desires to accomplish great things through the faith and works of his believing people. But we must stand in right relation to him, that when he speaks to us, we may hear and understand his voice. (White, *The Review and Herald,* November 17, 1910, par. 22)

Men and women in the church are privileged with the golden opportunity now to obtain an experience higher and holier, beautified with the attributes of Christ. They have a decided part to act in holding up the hands that are ready to fall. This is the work which must be done if the church is a living, active, working church. They must as a whole and as individuals tread Satan under their feet. The habits, the conversation, the daily life must be wholly consecrated on the Lord's side, and they must hold communion with God. He must be their divine Counselor, and there must be by the church as a whole and by its individual members a spirit of intercession and wrestling with our covenant-keeping God in behalf of themselves and also for the watchmen on the walls of Zion and the workers in the cause of God, that they may be clothed with the garments of salvation and may have at this time power to prevail with God, that many souls may be the fruits of their ministry. God will answer the earnest supplications that are sent to Him in faith. (White, *The Ellen G. White 1888 Materials*, pp. 755–756)

Tabernacles of Revelation—The Loud Cry Draws the Nations to Jesus (See also chapter 8)

In Revelation 18:1, we find the strong-voiced angel that appears to aid the three angels of Revelation 14, employing nearly the same wording of the second angel, but with a note on the range of coverage. "And after these things I saw another angel come down from heaven, having great power; and the earth was lightened with his glory."

The Revelation 18 angel is frequently spoken of as the glory, light, power, or loud voice of the third angel's message since it, like the third angel, warns against having any affiliation with Babylon at the risk of incurring the plagues of God's wrath. Then as a pitying Father, this angel makes a personal plea. It sounds around the earth with an urgency similar to that of the angels that were sent to rescue Lot from Sodom's destruction. "And I heard another voice from heaven, saying, Come out of her, my people, that ye be not partakers of her sins, and that ye receive not of her plagues" (v. 4).

In Zechariah 14, we found the compelling link of rain with the Feast of Tabernacles. Zechariah 10:1 adds the component of lightening the earth with the latter rain. "Ask the Lord for rain in the time of the latter rain. The LORD will make flashing clouds; He will give them showers of rain, Grass in the field for everyone" (NKJV). The heaviest rains are normally accompanied by the greatest displays of lightning. His laws came with light illuminating the character of God (see Exod. 20:18; Rev. 11:19), and these clouds, far from the dark ominous ones, are flashing with rays of brilliant light.

"When the Third Angel's Message shall go forth with a loud voice, the whole earth shall be lightened with His glory, the Holy Spirit is poured out upon His people. The revenue of glory has been accumulating for this closing work of the Third Angel's Message" (White, *Manuscript Releases*, vol. 1, p. 180).

"Arise, shine; for thy light is come, and the glory of the LORD is risen upon thee. For, behold, the darkness shall cover the earth, and gross darkness the people: but the LORD shall arise upon thee, and his glory shall be seen upon thee. And the Gentiles shall come to thy light, and kings to the brightness of thy rising" (Isa. 60:1–3).

> When God's people so fully separate themselves from evil that he can let the light of heaven rest upon them in rich measure, and shine forth from them to the world, then there will be fulfilled, more fully than it has ever been fulfilled in the past, the prophecy of Isaiah, in which the servant of God declared of the remnant church in the last days: "The Gentiles shall come to thy light, and kings to the brightness of thy rising. Lift up thine eyes round about, and see: all they gather themselves together, they come to thee: thy sons shall come from far, and thy daughters shall be nursed at thy side. Then thou shalt see, and flow together, and thine heart shall fear, and be enlarged; because the abundance of the sea shall be converted unto thee,

the forces of the Gentiles shall come unto thee." (White, *The Review and Herald*, March 31, 1910, par. 9)

Christ does not bid His followers strive to shine. He says, *Let your light shine*. If you have received the grace of God, the light is in you. Remove the obstructions, and the Lord's glory will be revealed. The light will shine forth to penetrate and dispel the darkness. You cannot help shining within the range of your influence. (White, *Christ's Object Lessons*, p. 420)

Those who have held the beginning of their confidence firm unto the end will be wide-awake during the time that the third angel's message is proclaimed with great power. (White, *Maranatha*, p. 218)

Now is the Time for Rain—The Dawning of Eternity

Present truth today places us between the second and third angels when they began in 1844 and when they finish with the loud voice of Revelation 18:1–5. The loud cry is the turning point for the imminence of the day of God looking ahead, because "the earth was lightened with his glory." Yes, that wonderful voice rolling through earth through human vessels corresponds with the time when the global latter rain is given.

> We must get ready for the latter rain. The earth is to be lighted with the glory of the third angel,—not a little corner only, but the whole earth. You may think that the work you are doing now is lost; but I tell you it is not lost. When the message shall go with a loud cry, those who hear the truth now will spring to the front and work with mighty power. (White, *The Review and Herald*, May 10, 1887, par. 20)

The prominent theme of the latter rain will be, as it has always been, the message of the cross which, when personally accepted and daily renewed, reconciles us to fellowship with our Maker. There is really no better qualification for the latter rain. "And I will pour upon the house of David, and upon the inhabitants of Jerusalem, the spirit of grace and of supplications: then they shall look upon me whom they have pierced, they shall mourn for him, as one mourneth for his only son, and shall be in bitterness for him, as one that is in bitterness for his firstborn" (Zech. 12:10).

"Come, and let us return unto the LORD: for he hath torn, and he will heal us; he hath smitten, and he will bind us up. After two days will he revive us: in the third day he will raise us up, and we shall live in his sight. Then shall we know, if we follow on to know the LORD: his going forth is prepared as the morning; and he shall come unto us as the rain, as the latter and former rain unto the earth" (Hosea 6:1–3). The book *The Great Controversy* quotes from this passage of Hosea and encapsulates how the former and latter rain compare:

> The work will be similar to that of the Day of Pentecost. As the "former rain" was given, in the outpouring of the Holy Spirit at the opening of the gospel, to cause the upspringing of the precious seed, so the "latter rain" will be given at its close for the ripening of the harvest. "Then shall we know, if we follow on to know the Lord: His going forth is prepared as the morning; and He shall come unto us as the rain, as the latter and former rain unto the earth." Hosea 6:3. "Be glad then, ye children of

Zion, and rejoice in the Lord your God: for He hath given you the former rain moderately, and He will cause to come down for you the rain, the former rain, and the latter rain." Joel 2:23. "In the last days, saith God, I will pour out of My Spirit upon all flesh." "And it shall come to pass, that whosoever shall call on the name of the Lord shall be saved." Acts 2:17, 21. (White, *The Great Controversy*, p. 611)

"Sow to yourselves in righteousness, reap in mercy; break up your fallow ground: for it is time to seek the LORD, till he come and rain righteousness upon you" (Hosea 10:12).

"And he shall be as the light of the morning, when the sun riseth, even a morning without clouds; as the tender grass springing out of the earth by clear shining after rain" (2 Sam. 23:4).

"And it shall come to pass, if ye shall hearken diligently unto my commandments which I command you this day, to love the LORD your God, and to serve him with all your heart and with all your soul, That I will give you the rain of your land in his due season, the first rain and the latter rain, that thou mayest gather in thy corn, and thy wine, and thine oil" (Deut. 11:13, 14).

"And they waited for me as for the rain; and they opened their mouth wide as for the latter rain" (Job 29:23).

"They shall fear thee as long as the sun & moon endure, throughout all generations. He shall come down like rain upon the mown grass: as showers that water the earth" (Ps. 72:5, 6; see also 1 Peter 1:24).

With suddenness the glory of the light of Isaiah 60:1–3 cascades into the second coming without a pause.

"Arise, shine; for thy light is come, and the glory of the Lord is risen upon thee." Isaiah 60:1. To those who go out to meet the Bridegroom is this message given. Christ is coming with power and great glory. He is coming with His own glory and with the

> glory of the Father. He is coming with all the holy angels with Him. While all the world is plunged in darkness, there will be light in every dwelling of the saints. They will catch the first light of His second appearing. The unsullied light will shine from His splendor, and Christ the Redeemer will be admired by all who have served Him. While the wicked flee from His presence, Christ's followers will rejoice. The patriarch Job, looking down to the time of Christ's second advent, said, "Whom I shall see for myself, and mine eyes shall behold, and not a stranger." Job 19:27, margin. (White, *Christ's Object Lessons*, p. 420–421)

God's call to arise and shine is in place before Christ's actual departure from the temple in heaven. The twelve apostles went out to meet the Bridegroom; then in a short time, by His power, gathered His scattered of the Gentiles from the extent of the entire known world (see Isaiah 60:2–3 and *Testimonies*, vol. 7, p. 62). In the end, the remnant repeats the same scenario, not only for an empire, but for every continent and isolated island. "He shall not fail nor be discouraged, till he have set judgment in the earth: and the isles shall wait for his law" (Isa. 42:4). When this work is completed, then Jesus leaves the temple.

> I saw angels hurrying to and fro in heaven. An angel with a writer's inkhorn by his side returned from the earth and reported to Jesus that his work was done, and the saints were numbered and sealed. Then I saw Jesus, who had been ministering before the ark containing the ten commandments, throw down the censer. He raised His hands, and with a loud voice said, *"It is done."* And all the angelic host laid off their crowns as Jesus made the solemn declaration, "He that is unjust, let him be unjust still: and he which is filthy, let him be filthy still: and he that is righteous, let him be righteous still: and he that is holy, let him be holy still."

Every case had been decided for life or death. While Jesus had been ministering in the sanctuary, the judgment had been going on for the righteous dead, and then for the righteous living. Christ had received His kingdom, having made the atonement for His people and blotted out their sins. The subjects of the kingdom were made up. The marriage of the Lamb was consummated. And the kingdom, and the greatness of the kingdom under the whole heaven, was given to Jesus and the heirs of salvation, and Jesus was to reign as King of kings and Lord of lords.

As Jesus moved out of the most holy place, I heard the tinkling of the bells upon His garment; and as He left, a cloud of darkness covered the inhabitants of the earth. (White, *Early Writings*, p. 279–280)

Prior to this, earth had progressively been plunging into spiritual darkness, yet still with hope.

Deepening Darkness of the Final Days Makes Brighter the Glory of God

Only the misapprehension of God, through the popular doctrines of devils such as eternal torment, keeps multitudes at an arm's length from God.

He causes "the light to shine out of darkness." 2 Corinthians 4:6. When "the earth was without form, and void, and darkness was upon the face of the deep," "the Spirit of God moved upon the face of the waters. And God said, Let there be light; and there was light." Genesis 1:2, 3. So in the night of spiritual darkness, God's word goes forth, "Let there be light." To His people He says, "Arise, shine; for thy light is come, and the glory of the Lord is risen upon thee." Isaiah 60:1.

Behold," says the Scripture, "the darkness shall cover the earth, and gross darkness the people; but the Lord shall arise upon thee, and His glory shall be seen upon thee." Isaiah 60:2.

It is the darkness of misapprehension of God that is enshrouding the world. Men are losing their knowledge of His character. It has been misunderstood and misinterpreted. At this time a message from God is to be proclaimed, a message illuminating in its influence and saving in its power. His character is to be made known. Into the darkness of the world is to be shed the light of His glory, the light of His goodness, mercy, and truth.

This is the work outlined by the prophet Isaiah in the words, "O Jerusalem, that bringest good tidings, lift up thy voice with strength; lift it up, be not afraid; say unto the cities of Judah, Behold your God! Behold, the Lord God will come with strong hand, and His arm shall rule for Him; behold, His reward is with Him, and His work before Him." Isaiah 40:9,10.

Those who wait for the Bridegroom's coming are to say to the people, "Behold your God." The last rays of merciful light, the last message of mercy to be given to the world, is a revelation of His character of love. The children of God are to manifest His glory. In their own life and character they are to reveal what the grace of God has done for them.

The light of the Sun of Righteousness is to shine forth in good works—in words of truth and deeds of holiness.

Christ, the outshining of the Father's glory, came to the world as its light. He came to represent God to men, and of Him it is written that He was anointed "with the Holy Ghost and with power," and "went about doing good." Acts 10:38. In the synagogue at Nazareth He said, "The Spirit of the Lord is upon Me, because He hath anointed Me to preach the gospel to the poor; He hath sent Me to heal the brokenhearted, to preach deliverance to the captives, and recovering of sight to the blind, to set at liberty them that are bruised, to preach the acceptable year of the Lord." Luke 4:18, 19. This was the work He commissioned His disciples to do. "Ye are the light of the world," He said. "Let your light so shine before men, that they may see your good works, and glorify your Father which is in heaven." Matthew 5:14, 16.

This is the work which the prophet Isaiah describes when he says, "Is it not to deal thy bread to the hungry, and that thou bring the poor that are cast out to thy house? when thou seest the naked, that thou cover him; and that thou hide not thyself from thine own flesh? Then shall thy light break forth as the morning, and thine health shall spring forth speedily; and thy righteousness shall go before thee; the glory of the Lord shall be thy [sic] reward." Isaiah 58:7, 8.

Thus in the night of spiritual darkness God's glory is to shine forth through His church in lifting up the bowed down and comforting those that mourn.

All around us are heard the wails of a world's sorrow. On every hand are the needy and distressed. It is ours to aid in relieving and softening life's hardships and misery....

...The message of hope and mercy is to be carried to the ends of the earth. Whosoever will, may reach forth and take hold of God's strength and make peace with Him, and he shall make peace. No longer are the heathen to be wrapped in midnight darkness. The gloom is to disappear before the bright beams of the Sun of Righteousness. The power of hell has been overcome. (White, *Christ's Object Lessons*, pp. 415–418)

The account of Elijah is rich in lessons applying to the hastening hour, which is the reason why we draw upon it often. An understanding of the latter rain is found through the experience of Elijah. After answering the prayers of Elijah, the rains are poured out upon a drought-stricken land after rescuing the cause of God in a time of spiritual emergency (see 1 Kings 17 and 18). His work of preparing Israel for salvation represents the remnant as God's saving instrument prior to the second coming (see James 5:17, 18), just as John the Baptist was Elijah's equivalent before the first coming.

> Verily I say unto you, Among them that are born of women there hath not risen a greater than John the Baptist: notwithstanding he that is least in the kingdom of heaven is greater than he. And from the days of John the Baptist until now the kingdom of heaven suffereth violence, and the violent take it by force. For all the prophets and the law prophesied until John. And if ye will receive it, this is Elias, which was for to come. He that hath ears to hear, let him hear. (Matthew 11:11–15)

"And as they came down from the mountain, Jesus charged them, saying, Tell the vision to no man, until the Son of man be risen again from the dead. And his disciples asked him, saying, Why then say the scribes that Elias must first come? And Jesus answered and said unto them, Elias truly shall first come, and restore all things" (Matt. 17:9–11; compare with Acts 3:21).

The characteristics of John's work gives further identity to the remnant's work: They are the door-openers to the visitation of God's power.

Now in the fifteenth year of the reign of Tiberius Caesar, Pontius Pilate being governor of Judaea, and Herod being tetrarch of Galilee, and his brother Philip tetrarch of Ituraea and of the region of Trachonitis, and Lysanias the tetrarch of Abilene, Annas and Caiaphas being the high priests, the word of God came unto John the son of Zacharias in the wilderness. And he came into all the country about Jordan, preaching the baptism of repentance for the remission of sins; As it is written in the book of the words of Esaias the prophet, saying, The voice of one crying in the wilderness, Prepare ye the way of the Lord, make his paths straight. Every valley shall be filled, and every mountain and hill shall be brought low; and the crooked shall be made straight, and the rough ways shall be made smooth; And all flesh shall see the salvation of God. (Luke 3:1–6)

According to Luke, the baptism of repentance (the door of faith to righteousness) prepares the way of the Lord, making straight His paths to earth. Then all flesh shall see the salvation of God. Revival of righteousness through the baptism of repentance taken up by Remnant members will unlock the door to the cascading of final events having the destiny of fulfilling the role of Elijah. "And it shall come to pass, that whosoever shall call on the name of the LORD shall be delivered: for in mount Zion and in Jerusalem shall be deliverance, as the LORD hath said, and in the remnant whom the LORD shall call" (Joel 2:32).

"Remember ye the law of Moses my servant, which I commanded unto him in Horeb for all Israel, with the statutes and judgments. Behold, I will send you Elijah the prophet before the coming of the great and dreadful day of the LORD" (Mal. 4:4, 5). Malachi affirms that this "Elijah" remembers the laws given to Moses, including the one law which had largely been ignored—namely, the fourth: "Remember the Sabbath day to keep it holy"—the commandment which identifies our Creator as the Lord of the commandments.

James also takes up the analogy of Elijah still to come. "Be patient therefore, brethren, unto the coming of the Lord. Behold, the husbandman waiteth for the precious fruit of the earth, and hath long patience for it, until he receive the early and latter rain. Be ye also patient; stablish your hearts: for the coming of the Lord draweth nigh" (James 5:7, 8). An all-important question is: When is the Lord drawing nigh? "…[when] the judge standeth before the door" (v. 9). This alludes to the imminent closing of the pre-advent judgment, post-1844. "Elijah…prayed earnestly that it would not rain; and it did not rain on the land for three years and six months. And he prayed again, and the heaven gave rain, and the earth produced its fruit" (vs. 17, 18, NKJV).

Incidentally, three and a half years in prophetic representation is equivalent to 1,260 years, the time span of the spiritual drought predicted in Daniel and Revelation. This was the Dark Ages of the former Roman Empire when ruled by the Papacy until 1798. True to prophecy, that age was soon after followed by Jesus' movement into the Most Holy Place for the Day of Atonement judgment. The three and a half years of drought of Elijah's time was followed by the showdown between the Baal followers and Jehovah's followers, ending with 450 unrepentant prophets of Baal purged out of Israel. Immediately after this came the cloudburst. This gives a sense that the judgment of today, while it may not end in the same literal way for the unrepentant tares, still follows the same the sequence—purification of the remnant through the Spirit, followed by the rain of the Spirit.

The new temple in the days of Solomon was dedicated on the Feast of Tabernacles, and the highlight of the feast was the king's special prayer.

> The time chosen for the dedication was a most favorable one—the seventh month, when the people from every part of the kingdom were accustomed to assemble at Jerusalem to

celebrate the Feast of Tabernacles. This feast was preeminently an occasion of rejoicing. The labors of the harvest being ended and the toils of the new year not yet begun, the people were free from care and could give themselves up to the sacred, joyous influences of the hour. (White, *Prophets and Kings*, p. 37)

When heaven is shut up, and there is no rain, because they have sinned against thee; if they pray toward this place, and confess thy name, and turn from their sin, when thou afflictest them: Then hear thou in heaven, and forgive the sin of thy servants, and of thy people Israel, that thou teach them the good way wherein they should walk, and give rain upon thy land, which thou hast given to thy people for an inheritance… What prayer and supplication soever be made by any man, or by all thy people Israel, which shall know every man the plague of his own heart, and spread forth his hands toward this house: Then hear thou in heaven thy dwelling place, and forgive, and do, and give to every man according to his ways, whose heart thou knowest; (for thou, even thou only, knowest the hearts of all the children of men;) (1 Kings 8:35–39)

"And it came to pass after many days, that the word of the LORD came to Elijah in the third year, saying, Go, show thyself unto Ahab; and I will send rain upon the earth…And Elijah came unto all the people, and said, How long halt ye between two opinions? if the LORD be God, follow him: but if Baal, then follow him. And the people answered him not a word" (1 Kings 18:1, 21). The response of the nation reflects the sleep that overtakes all the virgins waiting for the bridegroom.

One may wonder why there would ever be times of scarcity for the Word of God. About what were the Dark Ages? When there is a scarcity of seeking Him among a population at large, the choices are respected. In grieving, God knows that He can only oblige in order not to coerce humanity's free will. However, as revealed in prophecy, He foresaw a generation and future opportunity to achieve a massive awakening of multitudes, for which He has worked unceasingly behind the scenes. "…there is a sound of abundance of rain…the heaven was black with clouds and wind, and there was a great rain" (1 Kings 18:41, 45).

The Sealing Coincides with the Latter Rain

Revelation 7:1–4 and 14:1–5 bring to view the people who obtain the seal of God just before the door of salvation closes. "Hurt not the earth, neither the sea, nor the trees, till we have sealed the servants of our God in their foreheads" (7:3). Their state of readiness to receive this seal is marked by the second task—godly character. "And in their mouth was found no guile: for they are without fault before the throne of God" (14:5). As there is an early and latter rain, so there is also an early and latter seal. The seal signifies that a person is set to receive rain.

An early and latter judgment also tie into the seal and rain. The early church judgment prompted repentance in the upper room, preparing for the early seal and rain for the disciples in the aftermath of the cross. The subjects of that judgment were the children of Israel as a nation, which would have become the remnant had they not united to reject Jesus as their Messiah. The repentant who were baptized by John and later the disciples of Jesus enjoyed the early rain and seal (see Luke 24:49; Eph. 4:30). With the latter seal comes also the latter rain. "Not one of us will ever receive the seal of God while our characters have one spot or stain upon them. It is left with us…to cleanse the soul temple of every defilement. *Then the latter rain will fall upon us* as the early rain fell upon the disciples on the day of Pentecost" (White 1889, p. 214, emphasis added).

Not only does this quotation establish the inseparability of the seal and rain, it also prioritizes character restoration as our condition over outward religious activities. The work that moves the day forward will first be inward, then the outward will be showers of endless blessings. "The latter rain will come, and the blessing of God will fill *every soul that is purified from every defilement*. It is our work today to yield our souls to Christ, that we may be fitted for the time of refreshing from the presence of the Lord—fitted for the baptism of the Holy Spirit" (White 1892, p. 193, emphasis added).

> The time has come when we must expect the Lord to do great things for us. Our efforts must not flag or weaken. We are to grow in grace and in a knowledge of the Lord. *Before the work is closed up and the sealing of God's people is finished, we shall have the out-pouring of the Spirit of God*. Angels from heaven will be in our midst.…The present is the fitting up time for heaven, when we each must walk in full obedience to all the commandments of God. (White, *Manuscript Releases*, vol. 1, p. 175, emphasis added)

> We have now the invitations of mercy to become vessels unto honor, and then we need not worry about the latter rain; all we have to do is to keep the vessel clean and prepared and right side up, for the reception of the heavenly rain and keep praying, "Let the latter rain come into my vessel. Let the light of the glorious angel which unites with the third angel, shine upon me; give me a part in the work; let me sound the proclamation; let me be co-laborer with Jesus Christ." Thus seeking God, let me tell you, He is fitting you up all the time giving you His grace. You need not be worried. You need not be thinking that there is a special time coming when you are to be crucified; the time to be crucified is just now. Every day, every hour, self is to die; self is to be crucified, and then, when the time comes that the test shall come to God's people in earnest, the everlasting arms are around you. The angels of God make a wall of fire around

about and deliver you. All your self-crucifixion will not do any good then. It must come before the destiny of souls is decided. It is now that self is to be crucified, when there is work to do; when there is some use to be made of every entrusted capability. It is now that we are to empty and thoroughly cleanse the vessel of its impurity. It is now that we are to be made holy unto God. This is our work, this very moment. You are not to wait for any special period for a wonderful work to be done; it is today. I give myself to God today. (White, *Manuscript Releases*, vol. 1, pp. 179–180)

Keeping near God's guiding voice is truly our safeguard and light for our path as we approach the sealing of the church. "In these things I saw great danger; for if the mind is filled with other things, present truth is shut out, and there is no place in our foreheads for the seal of the living God" (White 1882, 58). "Those who come up to every point, and stand every test, and overcome, be the price what it may, have heeded the counsel of the True Witness, and *they will receive the latter rain, and thus be fitted for translation*" (White 1868, p. 187, emphasis added).

"These are they [the sealed] which follow the Lamb whithersoever he goeth. These were redeemed from among men, being the firstfruits unto God and to the Lamb." (Rev. 14:4, bracketed words derived from Rev. 7:2–4). The way this text is read in combination with the quotations above indicates that the sealed, during the latter rain, remain alive until they are translated when Christ appears. They "were redeemed from the earth" (14:3) and from among humanity (the living), rather than the grave.

Chapter 5

Hastening Window of Opportunity

Historicist Basis

The hastening window is based on historicism, a system for interpreting prophecy which was favored by the Protestant reformers. Historicism has enabled apocalyptic passages to be systematically deciphered. The picture that emerges is one of wonder and awe—a realization of a supernatural authorship that is beyond human thought; a perfect knowledge of all that is yet future, and in some instances, recorded

> *Historicism has enabled apocalyptic passages to be systematically deciphered. The picture that emerges is one of wonder and awe—a realization of a supernatural authorship that is beyond human thought; a perfect knowledge of all that is yet future, and in some instances, recorded for us thousands of years in advance.*

for us thousands of years in advance. Going to yet another level of God's unspeakable wisdom is the symbolic language expressed in most prophecies, such that they could only be understood when the time was right, and only by those under the enlightenment of His Spirit. The Bible's symbolism has also protected it from the danger of destruction by those identified in prophecies as enemies of God. Historicist-based interpretation provides a clear path of guidance in the midst of an apparent chaos that only intensifies until the end.

The historicist approach recognizes that primarily the visions of Daniel, Revelation, and passages from the gospels cover thousands of years of progressive fulfillment, reaching all the way to the earth made new, which is the final prophecy. Naturally, the best details are reserved for the last days, uncovering truth that reveals the place where we now find ourselves in earth's history and progressing toward what is imminently about to happen. What more could hold the attention of the onlooking universe and seekers on earth, that they may delight in God's present will for carrying out His hastening plans?

On the Prophetic Timeline, When Did the Hastening Window of Opportunity Open?

Although the last time prophecy, ending in 1844, removed prophetic delay, there may be concern about a possible delay due to the judgment of the dead, who naturally would have been the first to be reviewed according to the books of record, followed by the judgment of the living. Verses like 1 Peter 4:5 and others distinguish between the judgment of the dead and the living. The early members of the Adventist movement became aware that the transfer of the judgment from the dead to the living could occur at any time following the start of the antitypical Day of Atonement in 1844. Yet there is no known record of any concerns over delaying His return within their lifetime due to this judgment transitioning. The following quote was penned circa 1883:

> The angels of God in their messages to men represent time as very short. Thus it has always been presented to me. It is true that time has continued longer than we expected in the early days of this message. Our Saviour did not appear as soon as we hoped. But has the Word of the Lord failed? Never! It should be remembered that the promises and the threatenings of God are alike conditional. (White, *Evangelism*, p. 695)

True, although since the judgment of the dead had to be completed before Christ returned to earth, it need not be considered a delay. Perhaps God foreknew that the judgment of the dead would be completed well before the remnant movement could become a global influence with the everlasting gospel. How much more is this true today, when Adventism has had a notable global presence for more than half a century?

Several similar statements by Ellen White on the imminent transition of the judgment from the dead to the living were released around the important timeframe of the year 1888. The importance of that year will be discussed momentarily.

> We are living in the great antitypical day of atonement. Jesus is now in the heavenly sanctuary, making reconciliation for the sins of his people, and the judgment of the righteous dead has been going on almost forty years. How soon the cases of the living will come in review before this tribunal we know not; but we do know that we are living in the closing scenes of earth's history, standing, as it were, on the very borders of the eternal world. It is important that each of us inquire, How stands my case in the courts of Heaven? Will my sins be blotted out? Am

I defective in character, and so blinded to these defects by the customs and opinions of the world, that sin does not appear to me to be as exceedingly offensive to God as it really is? (White, *The Signs of the Times*, May 29, 1884, par. 3)

Within a few-year span revolving around the 1888 General Conference Session of Seventh-day Adventists, Ellen White wrote the following:

I address you who shall have this epistle brought before you, who are leaders, who may be termed princes among the people: "Be ye clean, that bear the vessels of the Lord" (Isaiah 52:11). Humble your souls before God. Jesus is in the sanctuary. We are in the great day of atonement, and *if the investigative judgment has not already commenced for the living, it will soon begin* and to how many are the words of the true witness applicable: "I know thy works, that thou hast a name that thou livest, and art dead. Be watchful, and strengthen the things which remain, that are ready to die: for I have not found thy works perfect before God. Remember therefore how thou hast received and heard, and hold fast, and repent. If therefore thou shalt not watch, I will come on thee as a thief, and thou shalt not know what hour I shall come upon thee" (Revelation 3:1–3). (White, *Manuscript Releases*, vol. 10, pp. 266–267, emphasis added)

Here is the work of our Intercessor, [on] the great antitypical day of atonement, where [the] work of judgment is going on with the dead. How soon will it begin with the living, when every one of our cases will pass in review before God? And let it be understood by you that if you do not [do] the work that God has given you, you will be weighed in the balances of the sanctuary and found wanting. To us who have this hope and faith *it is a dangerous thing to be putting off the day of God.* (White, *Sermons and Talks*, vol. 2, p. 27, emphasis added)

In 1844 our great High Priest entered the most holy place of the heavenly sanctuary, to begin the work of the investigative judgment. The cases of the righteous dead have been passing in review before God. When that work shall be completed, judgment is to be pronounced upon the living. How precious, how important are these solemn moments! Each of us has a case pending in the court of heaven. (White, *Selected Messages*, book. 1, p. 125)

We are a spectacle to the world, to angels, and to men. The whole universe is looking with inexpressible interest to see the closing work of the great controversy between Christ and Satan. At such a time as this, just as the great work of judging the living is to begin, shall we allow unsanctified ambition to take possession of the heart? What can be of any worth to us now except to be found loyal and true to the God of heaven? What is there of any real value in this world when we are on the very borders of the eternal world? (White, *Testimonies for the Church*, vol. 5, p. 526)

The judgment of the dead has been going on, and soon the judgment will begin upon the living, and every case will be decided. It will be known whose names are retained upon the book of life, and whose are blotted out. Every day the angels of God keep a record of the transactions of men, and these records stand open to the eyes of angels, and Christ, and God. Those who have manifested true repentance for sin, and by living faith in Christ are obedient to God's commandments, will have their names retained in the book of life, and they will be confessed before the Father and before the holy angels. Jesus will say, "They are mine; I have purchased them with my own blood." (White, *The Signs of the Times*, June 2, 1890, par. 4)

The last comparable statement was in 1898:

> When speaking to congregations, there is always before me the final judgment, which is to be held in the presence of the world, when the law of God's government is to be vindicated, His name glorified, His wisdom acknowledged and testified of as just to believers and unbelievers. This is not the judgment of one person, nor of a nation, but of a whole world of intelligent beings, of all orders, of all characters. The judgment takes place first upon the dead, then upon the living, then the whole universe will be assembled to hear the sentence. I feel as if I were in the presence of the whole universe of heaven, bearing my message for time and for eternity. (White, *Manuscript Releases*, vol. 8, p. 244)

That last sentence seems to indicate that the judgment may have already transferred to the living by 1898. It appears reasonable that from the turn of that century until now, there must have been a postponement of some kind. On the other hand, did God consider it more important to develop the organization with added elements such as medical and educational institutions? If there was postponement, was it caused by Darwinism, economic recession, Marxism, counterfeit religious movements, or something closer to home?

Is It Possible to Miss the Window of Opportunity?

At what other key times have the Lord's opportunities ever gone unnoticed by the lack of response from His people? Near the end of the seventy weeks of years which predicted the year of the first advent of the Messiah, there was a star of wonder hovering over Bethlehem, but the sign was not recognized by the children of Israel. It was the Gentile wise men who saw the fulfillment of prophecy. Only they and a handful of shepherds were granted the honor of welcoming the Monarch of the universe to earth.

At the first opportunity to cross over the Jordan, the shallow river became an impassable wall for that generation of Israelites. The tendency of God's people for being stopped by walls of their own imagining is as strong today as it was throughout recorded history. Skepticism is not always a bad thing, but it easily goes too far, especially when good news seems too good to be true.

> *The tendency of God's people for being stopped by walls of their own imagining is as strong today as it was throughout recorded history.*

Postponement of the Latter 1800s

The year 1888 is probably second most memorable year, next to 1844, in the progress of the Adventist movement. From the perspective of an average assessment of the events of that year, the impression is that 1888 was not known as a milestone of success, but a stinging retreat from the adversary. While 1844 was a disappointment for the believers, it held the deepest interest for heaven's host; but of 1888, it can be viewed as a reversal—a disappointment in heaven's sight. A most far-reaching disruption on the road to Christ's coming is considered to have occurred in 1888, resulting from discord and disunion among Adventist leadership. These troubles came to a valley of decision at the church's General Conference Session held in Minneapolis, Minnesota.

During the years leading up to the golden opportunity, spiritual Israel began to settle into entrenchment rather than advancement to higher ground.

> I know that a work must be done for the people, or many will not be prepared to receive the light of the angel sent down from heaven to lighten the whole earth with his glory. Do not think that you will be found as vessels unto honor in the time of the latter rain, to receive the glory of God, if you are lifting up your souls unto vanity, speaking perverse things, in secret cherishing roots of bitterness brought from the conference at Minneapolis [in 1888]. The frown of God will certainly be upon every soul who cherishes and nurtures these roots of dissension, and possesses a spirit so unlike the Spirit of Christ. (White, *The Ellen G. White 1888 Materials*, p. 442)

Every revival movement of the Holy Spirit begins with new or revived Scripture enlightenment given by His messengers. This is true of the end-time window of opportunity when new or restored Bible instruction comes into view. The powers of darkness, ever aware of such developments, stand ready to repress opportunity with outbreaks of opposition, both externally and internally.

Rather than getting into the details and exchanges that took place at the 1888 meetings, its general outcome can be summarized by a few statements from Ellen White. She lived through this experience and personally heard the messengers, elders E. J. Waggoner and A. T. Jones.

> We are impressed that this gathering will be the most important meeting you have ever attended. This should be a period of earnestly seeking the Lord, and humbling your hearts before Him. I hope you will regard this as a most precious opportunity to pray and counsel together; and if the injunction of the apostle to esteem others better than ourselves is carefully heeded, then you can in humility of mind, with the spirit of Christ, search the scriptures carefully to see what is truth. (White, *The Ellen G. White 1888 Materials*, p. 38)

> The Lord in His great mercy sent a most precious message to his people through Elders Waggoner and Jones. This message was to bring more prominently before the world the uplifted Saviour, the sacrifice for the sins of the whole world. It presented justification through faith in the Surety; it invited the people to receive the righteousness of Christ, which is made manifest in obedience to all the commandments of God. Many had lost sight of Jesus. They needed to have their eyes directed to His divine person, His merits, and His changeless love for the human family. All power is given into His hands, that he may dispense rich gifts unto men, imparting the priceless gift of His own righteousness to the helpless human agent. *This is the message that God commanded to be given to the world. It is the third angel's message, which is to be proclaimed with a loud voice, and attended with the outpouring of His Spirit in a large measure.* (White, *The Ellen G. White 1888 Materials*, pp. 1336–1337, emphasis added)

That statement gives a clear sense of the second-coming potential that existed then. Notice the one major thought, the righteousness of Christ, as it is widely adopted by His repentant people, will be followed by the next major event, "the outpouring of His Spirit in a large measure." What was the actual outcome of the conference?

> The conference at Minneapolis was the golden opportunity for all present to humble the heart before God and to welcome Jesus as the great Instructor, but the stand taken by some at that meeting proved their ruin. They have never seen clearly since, and they never will, for they persistently cherish the spirit that prevailed there, a wicked, criticizing, denunciatory spirit. Yet since that meeting, abundant light and evidence has been graciously given, that all might understand what is truth. (White, *The Ellen G. White 1888 Materials*, pp. 1125–1126)

The 1888 generation has come and gone, yet many Calebs and Joshuas were registered in heaven as resting in the Lord, and their works do follow them (see Rev. 14:13). They faithfully gave a "good report" in favor of the righteousness of Christ, but they were only a small minority of the congregation (more on this later).

The next statements speak of the very scenario which, according to prophecy, indicates that the second coming was to be imminently expected, yet apparently postponed. Notice that the timeframe for these statements is within the range of about a decade during the 1880s and 1890s. Compare these with the judgment-of-the-living statements above, written between 1884 and 1898. From the context, they suggest that Christ was ready to return within that timeframe. All other conditions were in place, including the growing threat of Sunday-law legislation, Satan's response to the remnant coming near the border of Pentecost power.

> The prophetic word shows clearly *that we are living near the close of this world's history, and that we may soon expect the coming of the Son of man in the clouds of Heaven.* As the Israelites journeyed toward the earthly Canaan, so are we pressing onward to reach the heavenly Canaan. The history of their backslidings is repeated among the people of God today. (White, *The Signs of the Times*, May 26, 1881, par. 17, emphasis added)

In 1885, Ellen White stated, "In this age of the world, as the scenes of earth's history are soon to close and we are about to enter upon the time of trouble such as never was, the fewer the marriages contracted, the better for all, both men and women." A few years later, she wrote the following:

> We are standing on the threshold of great and solemn events. Prophecy is fast fulfilling. The Lord is at the door. There is soon to open before us a period of overwhelming interest to

all living. The controversies of the past are to be revived; new controversies will arise. The scenes to be enacted in our world are not yet even dreamed of. Satan is at work through human agencies. Those who are making an effort to change the Constitution and secure a law enforcing Sunday observance little realize what will be the result. A crisis is just upon us. (White, *Testimonies for the Church*, vol. 5 p. 753)

A great crisis awaits the people of God. A crisis awaits the world. The most momentous struggle of all the ages is just before us....The question of enforcing Sunday observance has become one of national interest and importance. We well know what the result of this movement will be. But are we ready for the issue? Have we faithfully discharged the duty which God has committed to us of giving the people warning of the danger before them?...

If popery or its principles shall again be legislated into power, the fires of persecution will be rekindled against those who will not sacrifice conscience and the truth in deference to popular errors. This evil is on the point of realization. (White, *Maranatha*, p. 131)

From the search that generated these statements, it seems that during much of the 1880s, the second coming was written as an imminent expectation for the Adventists of that time. After that, she is found lamenting of the apparent postponing of the Lord's return, and the dates of these expressions are found mostly during the years just after the turn of the century. In reading the following statements, you will eventually notice a pivot.

Brethren, we have little time in which to work. Certainly we need to stop complaining about each other, and lay our whole hearts open before God, that we may receive the Holy Spirit. Years ago the time came for the Holy Spirit to descend in a special manner upon God's earnest, self-sacrificing workers. The Lord will greatly bless His tried and chosen ones if they will cooperate with Him. When the Holy Spirit came down in the day of Pentecost, it was like a rushing, mighty wind. It was given in no stinted measure; for it filled all the place where the disciples were sitting. So will it be given to us when our hearts are prepared to receive it. (White, *Manuscript Releases*, vol. 1, pp. 175–176)

Had Adventists, after the great disappointment in 1844, held fast their faith and followed on unitedly in the opening providence of God, receiving the message of the third angel and in the power of the Holy Spirit proclaiming it to the world, they would have seen the salvation of God, the Lord would have wrought mightily with their efforts, the work would have been completed, and Christ would have come ere this to receive His people to their reward. But in the period of doubt and uncertainty that followed the disappointment, many of the advent believers yielded their faith…Thus the work was hindered, and the world was left in darkness. Had the whole Adventist body united upon the commandments of God and the faith of Jesus, how widely different would have been our history!

It was not the will of God that the coming of Christ should be thus delayed. God did not design that His people, Israel, should wander forty years in the wilderness. He promised to lead them directly to the land of Canaan, and establish them there a holy, healthy, happy people. But those to whom it was first preached, went not in "because of unbelief." Their hearts were filled with murmuring, rebellion, and hatred, and He could not fulfill His covenant with them.

For forty years did unbelief, murmuring, and rebellion shut out ancient Israel from the land of Canaan. The same sins have delayed the entrance of modern Israel into the heavenly Canaan. In neither case were the promises of God at fault. It is the unbelief, the worldliness, unconsecration, and strife among the Lord's professed people that have kept us in this world of sin and sorrow so many years….

…We may have to remain here in this world because of insubordination many more years, as did the children of Israel; but for Christ's sake, His people should not add sin to sin by charging God with the consequence of their own wrong course of action. (White, *Evangelism*, pp. 695–696)

Had the purpose of God been carried out by His people in giving to the world the message of mercy, Christ would, ere this, have come to the earth, and the saints would have received their welcome into the city of God.

I know that if the people of God had preserved a living connection with Him, if they had obeyed His Word, they would today be in the heavenly Canaan.

If every watchman on the walls of Zion had given the trumpet a certain sound, the world might ere this have heard the message of warning. But the work is years behind. While men have slept, Satan has stolen a march upon us. (White, *Evangelism*, p. 694)

Once hastening became available shortly after 1844 and all of Ellen White's delay statements above had been written, it is noteworthy that she continued to write with a sense of imminence. What a privilege it is to be alive today, yet it is sobering to consider that this was made possible by over 100 years of delay, which might have been over 100 years of living in the heavenly Canaan instead of this doomed planet with continued heartache.

> The end is near, stealing upon us stealthily, imperceptibly, like the noiseless approach of a thief in the night. May the Lord grant that we shall no longer sleep as do others, but that we shall watch and be sober. The truth is soon to triumph gloriously, and all who now choose to be laborers together with God, will triumph with it. The time is short; the night soon cometh when no man can work. (White, *Evangelism*, p. 692)

Before that night ever comes, God's house must first be filled. Of course, failing to get through during that narrow opportunity, which likely opened in the late 1800s, has allowed for the hedging up arrangements put in place by Satan. He had enough time and opportunity to implement them while the remnant was caught up in theological discord and issues allowing our opportunity to close for that time. Whether it is open again today is largely in our hands by grace. It is difficult to comprehend how it is that God hangs so much of the world's destiny upon the movements of God's people.

> The hindrances to strength and success are far greater from the church itself than from the world. Unbelievers have a right to expect that those who profess to be keeping the commandments of God and the faith of Jesus, will do more than any other class to promote and honor, by their consistent lives, by their godly example and their active influence, the cause which they represent. But how often have the professed advocates of the truth proved the greatest obstacle to its advancement! The unbelief indulged, the doubts expressed, the darkness cherished, encourage the presence of evil angels, and open the way for the accomplishment of Satan's devices. (White, *Last Day Events*, p. 156)

The stolen march referenced above has resulted in decades of delay as the tables were turned; then followed world wars, the Great Depression, socialism, communism, the "science" of evolution, religious extremism, counterfeit Christian systems, etc. They have set up their barriers against billions to knowing the everlasting gospel. "For all nations have drunk of the wine of the wrath of [Babylon's] fornication" (Rev. 18:3). New approaches and better clarity in teaching the truth had to be developed to counteract the new barriers.

Heaven is not yet a present reality, but a past generation's folly is the present generation's opportunity to have been born. With this privilege, while living when no fixed delays remain, what then shall we do? Peter's call to hasten has passed on to us. Opportunity now rings again because recently closed nations like various remnants of former Soviet Union, China, and Vietnam, are now seeing phenomenal Christian liberties. There have been recent reports that the Lord is working to open up Islamic nations as well.

By 1901, the new light was still being disregarded, as noted in the next passage. The tone then immediately changes as a wonderful scene describing what fulfillment of the overcoming, righteousness-by-faith goal would look like.

> One day at noon I was writing of the work that might have been done at the last General Conference [1901] if the men in positions of trust had followed the will and way of God. Those who have had great light have not walked in the light. The meeting was closed, and the break was not made. Men did not humble themselves before the Lord as they should have done, and the Holy Spirit was not imparted.
>
> I had written thus far when I lost consciousness, and I seemed to be witnessing a scene in Battle Creek.
>
> We were assembled in the auditorium of the Tabernacle. Prayer was offered, a hymn was sung, and prayer was again offered. Most earnest supplication was made to God. The meeting was marked by the presence of the Holy Spirit. The work went deep, and some present were weeping aloud.

One arose from his bowed position and said that in the past he had not been in union with certain ones and had felt no love for them, but that now he saw himself as he was. With great solemnity he repeated the message to the Laodicean church: "'Because thou sayest, I am rich, and increased with goods, and have need of nothing.' In my self-sufficiency this is just the way I felt," he said. "'And knowest not that thou art wretched, and miserable, and poor, and blind, and naked.' I now see that this is my condition. My eyes are opened. My spirit has been hard and unjust. I thought myself righteous, but my heart is broken, and I see my need of the precious counsel of the One who has searched me through and through. Oh, how gracious and compassionate and loving are the words, 'I counsel thee to buy of Me gold tried in the fire, that thou mayest be rich; and white raiment, that thou mayest be clothed, and that the shame of thy nakedness do not appear; and anoint thine eyes with eyesalve, that thou mayest see.'" Revelation 3:17, 18.

The speaker turned to those who had been praying, and said: "We have something to do. We must confess our sins, and humble our hearts before God." He made heartbroken confessions and then stepped up to several of the brethren, one after another, and extended his hand, asking forgiveness. Those to whom he spoke sprang to their feet, making confession and asking forgiveness, and they fell upon one another's necks, weeping. The spirit of confession spread through the entire congregation. It was a Pentecostal season. God's praises were sung, and far into the night, until nearly morning, the work was carried on.

The following words were often repeated, with clear distinctness: "As many as I love, I rebuke and chasten: be zealous therefore, and repent. Behold, I stand at the door, and knock: if any man hear My voice, and open the door, I will come in to him, and will sup with him, and he with Me." Verses 19, 20.

No one seemed to be too proud to make heartfelt confession, and those who led in this work were the ones who had influence, but had not before had courage to confess their sins.

There was rejoicing such as never before had been heard in the Tabernacle.

Then I aroused from my unconsciousness, and for a while could not think where I was. My pen was still in my hand. The words were spoken to me: *"This might have been.* All this the Lord was waiting to do for His people. All heaven was waiting to be gracious." I thought of where we might have been had thorough work been done at the last General Conference, and agony of disappointment came over me as I realized that what I had witnessed was not a reality. (White, *Testimonies for the Church*, vol. 8, pp. 104–106)

One unseen implication of the 1888 message is that the golden moment to hasten Jesus' return during that era had arrived—possibly because the judgment of the dead had concluded soon after that year. We find this suggested by the timing of the previous quotations. With no further restraints remaining then, heaven immediately bears good news to the church via the gift of advancing Scripture light pertaining to Christ, who is blotting out our sins for the time of refreshing. This light was to supply that vital piece of the last message to humans, that they may put on the garment of Christ's righteousness.

Determining a Successful Window Closing

Generally speaking, it is Matthew 24:14 that would seem to close the window, but the turning point is sooner. From the first moment of the outpouring, the judgment window closes initially for the existing church. After that, world coverage of the gospel through the Elijah remnant results in the sealing, person by person (see Rev. 7:3), among the remainder of God's children in Babylon.

In other words, for all intents and purposes, a successful hastening window closes, not at the close of global probation, but earlier, at the start of the second global outpouring, the moment when His people so fully connect with God (are sealed) that nothing delays the second-coming conditions from being fulfilled from that point onward. God's last hastening work is then fully engaged, and He carries His people to the finished work.

There is a role exchange that takes place at the crossing of this outpouring threshold into eternity, assuring that the saints who partake in the outpouring live on through the remaining events until the second advent. Then Isaiah 60:22 is realized: "I the LORD will hasten it in his time." He still uses human vessels until the close, but during the outpouring, they are under such a complete baptism of the Holy Spirit that they are as standing still while the Lord fights for them (see Exod. 14:14). Though afflicted, they may say with Paul, "And He said unto me, My grace is sufficient for thee: for my strength is made perfect in weakness. Most gladly therefore will I rather glory in my infirmities, that the power of Christ may rest upon me" (2 Cor. 12:9).

As a result of this level of grace, a corresponding level of Christlikeness will transform the saints as they enter into the Elijah/John the Baptist experience—the earth-lightening angel of Revelation 18 that will captivate the populations of earth. The coming of Christ most definitely depends on this high spiritual note. In a practical sense, this is the essence of the second Pentecost, when God can so entirely employ His people, through their consent of faith surrender, that He carries out the burden of the final labors. The three angels' messages then, with comparative ease, saturate the globe and ripen the global harvest for ingathering (the fourth task).

Given these possibilities today, the choice is clear between living by an imminent hope or one that is far off in the future. Ezekiel had some thoughts on this:

The word of the LORD came to me: "Son of man, what is this proverb you have in the land of Israel: 'The days go by and every vision comes to nothing'? Say to them, 'This is what the Sovereign LORD says: I am going to put an end to this proverb, and they will no longer quote it in Israel.' Say to them, 'The days are near when every vision will be fulfilled. For there will be no more false visions or flattering divinations among the people of Israel. But I the Lord will speak what I will, and it shall be fulfilled without delay. For in your days, you rebellious people, I will fulfill whatever I say, declares the Sovereign LORD.'" The word of the LORD came to me: "Son of man, the Israelites are saying, 'The vision he sees is for many years from now, and he prophesies about the distant future.' "Therefore say to them, 'This is what the Sovereign LORD says: None of my words will be delayed any longer; whatever I say will be fulfilled, declares the Sovereign LORD.'" (Ezekiel 12:21–28, NIV)

The Other Window Alternative

The alternative during this golden window is when an overall response to His wedding invitation wavers and begins to fade. If this present opportunity passes, then the window closing would last until a later opportunity opens during another generation. Satanic opposition is alert to missed opportunity, and if history repeats itself, he may be able to again quickly move in, swallowing large populations into gospel-inaccessible captivity which would remain until God's spiritual workings again begin to unravel the tangled web.

Therefore, if His people today are to have a quickening role, a specific identity would be needed to change the present trend to an accelerated one; an identity against which the powers of darkness are exerting their greatest opposition.

Chapter 6

The Last Generation Identity

To the children of God today are granted the invitation and ownership for making a difference as to when His glory will be seen. "It is high time that we were awake out of sleep, that we seek the Lord with all the heart, and I know He will be found of us. I know that all heaven is at our command. Just as soon as we love God with all our hearts and our neighbor as ourselves, God will work through us. How shall we stand in the time of the latter rain" (White 1990, p. 60)?

Each member is at this time offered the power of one more weight upon the balance in favor of living to witness Jesus coming in the clouds. The consent of Adam and Eve had power over whether *their* earth would plunge into death and despair. His respect of the will of the bride applies to closing events. With just an overall united consent, the power of the Holy Spirit will aid the weakness of humanity, which in the past has leaned towards delay (see 2 Peter 3:9) rather than expedition (see v. 12).

They Were All with One Accord

"Before the final visitation of God's judgments upon the earth there will be among the people of the Lord such a revival of primitive godliness as has not been witnessed since apostolic times" (White 1911, p. 464).

"Jesus is at work through His instruments to gather and unite. Satan works through His instruments to scatter and divide" (White 1868, p. 332).

"This work can be accomplished only by *the whole church* acting their part under the guidance and in the power of Christ" (White 1904, p. 47).

In measures, God has released rain revival in various times and places, such as during early Adventism. By comparison, the latter rain will be both global and uninterrupted until the last wedding guest has entered the banquet. At what moment does the rain go from scattered and small to global? That may be the question of the millennium, one that is worth every detail we can uncover.

We have found that the chief answer is the second task, a sanctified congregation (see Joel 2:15) How/when will the church ever be righteous enough to satisfy their wedding garment condition? Will the Lord require entire church sanctification?

The Elect of the Remnant

"Elect according to the foreknowledge of God the Father, through sanctification of the Spirit, unto obedience and sprinkling of the blood of Jesus Christ: Grace unto you, and peace, be multiplied" (1 Peter 1:2).

> In my dream a sentinel stood at the door of an important building, and asked every one who came for entrance, "Have ye received the Holy Ghost?" A measuring-line was in his hand, and only very, very few were admitted into the building. "Your size as a human being is nothing," he said. "But if you have reached the full stature of a man in Christ Jesus, according to the knowledge you have had, you will receive an appointment to sit with Christ at the marriage supper of the Lamb; and through the eternal ages, you will never cease to learn of the blessings granted in the banquet prepared for you. (White, *Selected Messages*, book 1, pp. 109–110)

Since the dawn of the early church until today, when two billion or so have identified themselves with the Christian faith, it isn't a secret that only a small portion believe and receive all that God offers. The minority referenced in 1 Peter 1:2 may be the elect referred to in Matthew 24:24 whom the false Christs and false prophets would love to deceive if possible. They are the elect within the remnant who likely may not even know this themselves until they are experiencing the rains. His elect followers persevere until the end, including many who return after some time away. It is important to emphasize that this elect does not go out from the remnant, but remains within and supports the whole.

These people accept Elijah's challenge of leading Israel to repentance, and like Moses are asking, "Who is on the Lord's side" (Exod. 32:26)? Earlier it was mentioned that another Elijah is expected just before the final day of the Lord, and it must be the elect among the congregation. (see Mal. 4:5).

Is the church completely pure before it can give the loud cry of Revelation 18:1–4, the core message during the time of the latter rain? Even though Joel 2:16 says, "sanctify the congregation," would that mean the entire congregation of total membership, or a certain portion?

> The old standard bearers knew what it was to wrestle with God in prayer, and to enjoy the outpouring of His Spirit. But these are passing off from the stage of action; and who are coming up to fill their places? How is it with the rising generation? Are they converted to God? Are we awake to the work that is going on in the heavenly sanctuary, or are we waiting for some compelling power to come upon the church before we shall arouse? Are we hoping to see the whole church revived? That time will never come." (White, *Selected Messages*, book 1, p. 122)

Matthew 13:24–30 helps to clarify this. The wheat and tares grow together until the end, so evidently the Lord will "accommodate" some in the church who are lacking a wedding garment, yet not so many as to hinder His finishing plan. Though an individual Christian is required to overcome all sin captivity, the church as a whole, which inherits the promises, is going to have a few who remain tares. In farm fields, most tares are fairly prickly and annoying, but as long as the crops are kept nourished and robust, the noxious spread of the tares can be diminished.

> I was pointed back, and saw that in every important move, every decision made or point gained by God's people, some have arisen to carry matters to extremes, and to move in an extravagant manner, which has disgusted unbelievers, distressed God's people, and brought the cause of God into disrepute. The people whom God is leading out in these last days, will be troubled with just such things. But much evil will be avoided if the ministers of Christ will be of one mind, united in their plans of action, and united in effort. If they will stand together, sustain one another, and faithfully reprove and rebuke wrong, they will soon cause it to wither. (White, *Testimonies for the Church*, vol. 1, pp. 212–213)

Simply a Majority Rules

For what portion of the membership is God seeking in order to give the full showers of the Holy Spirit? More than a handful? Half? Or a specific number?

The following indicates why God's outpouring was unlikely to occur during the turn of the nineteenth century. "It is a solemn statement that I make to the church, that not one in twenty whose names are registered upon the church books are prepared to close their earthly history, and would be as verily without God and without hope in the world as the common sinner" (White 1992, p. 172).

In answer to the question above, we have this statement:

> The great outpouring of the Spirit of God, which lightens the whole earth with His glory, will not come until we have *an enlightened people*, that know by experience what it means to be laborers together with God. When we have entire, *wholehearted consecration* to the service of Christ, God will recognize the fact by an outpouring of His Spirit without measure; but this will not be while *the largest portion* of the church are not laborers together with God. (White, *Last Day Events*, p. 193, emphasis added)

Wouldn't "largest portion" be the same as a majority? "Enlightened" and "wholehearted consecration" are synonymous with genuine righteousness by faith. Therefore, "entire" or "whole" is recognized as such by the combined character of the largest portion. In the past, the elect has been a minority in the church, almost with a settled expectation. A church with a minority elect that has become a majority elect is a church that is reckoned as consecrated.

> A church with a minority elect that has become a majority elect is a church that is reckoned as consecrated.

The next statement, which comes a couple paragraphs before the previous one, further reflects upon the second task—righteousness by faith: "The latter rain will come, and the blessing of God will fill every soul that is *purified from every defilement*. It is our work today to *yield our souls to Christ*, that we may be fitted for the time of refreshing from the presence of the Lord—fitted for the baptism of the Holy Spirit" (emphasis added).

The following statement describes the spirit of those under the movement of His Spirit: "Every truly converted soul will be intensely desirous to bring others from the darkness of error into the marvelous light of the righteousness of Jesus Christ" (White 1952, p. 59).

Therefore, when those who gather and unite to see eye to eye make up the largest number of the church, then the greater weight of movement will be to accomplish God's perfect will. In case the membership feels content to leave this work with the ministers, they should notice another passage that makes crystal clear how important every individual role is. "The work of God in this earth can never be finished until the men and women comprising our church membership rally to the work and unite their efforts with those of ministers and church officers" (White 1909, p. 117).

"God will work a work in our day that but few anticipate. He will raise up and exalt among us those who are taught rather by the unction of his Spirit, than by the outward training of scientific institutions. These facilities are not to be despised or condemned; they are ordained of God, but they can furnish only the exterior qualifications" (White 1889, p. 82).

The joyful outcome of the judgment is a transition from a people mostly unprepared to a people mostly prepared to see God. The citizenship is brought up to what is in practicality the whole church, as represented by a majority. This is the basis for the closing movements of Jesus—not on how the bride now appears, but on how she's going to appear (see Rev. 19:7).

With this in consideration, each member's personal, communion-level righteousness truly contributes toward shortening the time by another measure.

At what rate does the third angel's message become the loud cry of Revelation 18? "The work of this angel [in Rev. 18:1] comes in at the right time to join in the last great work of the third angel's message as it swells to a loud cry" (White 1882, p. 277). This is not intermittent or sporadic. As there is no longer a necessary delay by that time, the acceleration of the "swell" depends on a united consent.

"We stand as the remnant people in these last days to promulgate the truth and swell the cry of the third angel's wonderful distinct message, giving the trumpet a certain sound. Eternal truth, which we have adhered to from the beginning, *is to be maintained in all its increasing importance to the close of probation"* (White 1990, p. 314).

The sanctified people of God have been drinking from the river of life, starting from the early and small rains in scattered places; but globally speaking, the latter rain is reserved for the time when they have become a majority. This is the church's threshold of no turning back when the Lord stands at the door of the temple.

Chapter 7

The Lord Draweth Nigh (James 5:7-9)

Threshold Crossing in Flight History

While this manuscript material was in progress, an episode of *Nova* aired, providing a number of surprising analogies and featuring probably the most ambitious achievement of flight since the Wright Brothers first lifted off the ground (Nova Online, http://1ref.us/nx [accessed 08/16/2018]).

The ultimate purpose for experimental pursuits of speed was the space race of the superpowers during the Cold War as they sought to conquer the cosmos through human resources and ingenuity. In the era of American invention, few enterprises have been as ambitious as air/space travel, when each engineering advance was a springboard to the next, with no end in sight. During the post-WWII years,

> *In the era of American invention, few enterprises have been as ambitious as air/space travel, when each engineering advance was a springboard to the next, with no end in sight.*

flight technology was steaming ahead until a great, invisible wall was encountered.

Brigadier General Chuck Yeager was the test pilot who first conducted a controlled flight past the sound barrier. Until the late 1940's, no one had been able to reach the speed of sound without losing control or their plane breaking up in the air. Pilots either perished or barely escaped because they managed to slow their craft enough to regain control, before hitting the ground.

Regarding the time of war, when the Nazis were getting ahead in flight speed with the first jet engine, De Beeler said, "There were considerable bouts of pessimism. That was the environment at that present time…" that it just couldn't be done. And this hopelessness trickled "…down to the designers even themselves. Well, there were a lot of people that said it was impossible. And that's when they talked about the sonic wall. The sonic wall, that means like a brick wall. And a lot of people accepted that." Then De E. Beeler, one of the aeronautical engineers, said, "let's go step by step and use all the tools and knowledge in Europe, anywhere we could find it, and put it together and see what we would come up with."

There was an impasse with that sound barrier. Do we have our own barrier? There are frequent resignations about Christ returning in our generation. Many believe it is allegedly impossible because there is still way too much work to do. On the other hand, faith says that we're living at a time when every remaining delay can be eliminated with the help of God. The cooperation on our part that breaks open the barrier is the faith level of daily communion with God. That alone is the opportunity to hear God's plans and receive His power—the same experience Jesus and Elijah had.

Do we sometimes get a sense that the second coming and heaven are like a brick wall? It's not that we doubt these pillars of truth, but after looking at appearances and hearing the statistics that tell us how far we are from covering the world with His message, then rationally speaking, it must be some future generation that finishes it long after we are gone.

In this sound barrier account, what was the problem with the sonic wall?

"Capt. Eric Brown: There was a huge amount of vibration juddering through the aircraft. As you got closer to the speed of sound, each bite beyond a certain limit was fraught with the possibility of disaster."

"Stacy Keach (Narrator): It was during World War II that pilots first experienced the problem of flying too close to the speed of sound. It happened when fighter planes went into steep attacking dives. Some went so fast they were buffeted by forces they could not control."

Close to the speed of sound, the sound waves were compacting on the aircraft which was emitting the noise and the impact was called shock waves. Because of the concentration of energy at that speed, it hammered the plane and froze the controls.

Flying past the sound barrier is comparable to completing the evangelism task that sets us up for translation, but because of turmoil (from the devil) occurring near the speed of sound (of God's voice), we may feel pessimism to the point of defeat—that maybe it is impossible to go any faster, even though we today are called upon to accelerate the day (see 2 Pet. 3:3, 12; Heb. 10:25, 35–37).

Speaking of the papacy, with support from the serpent (see Rev. 13:4), and its response to the good news getting noticed in the world, Daniel writes, "But news from the east and the north shall trouble him; therefore he shall go out with great fury to destroy and annihilate many" (11:44, NKJV). When the gospel takes off in power, Satan will throw everything possible at it because by then, nothing can stop it. However, for now, the tactic of darkness is to keep us from fulfilling our role—being a church in the full stature of Christ, with readiness for the latter rain, and becoming the angel of Revelation 18, joining the third angel of Revelation 14:9–11.

> If the church will put on the robe of Christ's righteousness, withdrawing from all allegiance with the world, there is before her the dawn of a bright and glorious day. God's promise to

her will stand fast forever. He will make her an eternal excellency, a joy of many generations. Truth, passing by those who despise and reject it, will triumph. Although at times apparently retarded, its progress has never been checked. When the message of God meets with opposition, He gives it additional force, that it may exert greater influence. Endowed with divine energy, it will cut its way through the strongest barriers and triumph over every obstacle. (White, *The Acts of the Apostles*, p. 601)

Peter, in his first epistle, states that the wrath of Satan may touch us, but the same is used by God for our good, serving to perfect, establish, and strengthen us, while irresistibly persuading others around us (see 5:7–10; also Matt. 5:16).

"Stacy Keach (Narrator): No one knew what happened to planes as they approached the speed of sound. For some reason, they began to behave unpredictably. Pilots began to speak of an impenetrable wall to high speed flight, a sound barrier. No official records were kept, but some wartime pilots simply disappeared during high speed dives."

So they worked on the problem with the plane on the ground, putting it in a wind tunnel in which they could move air near the speed of sound. But that posed some problems.

"Stacy Keach (Narrator): In the 1940s, wind tunnels were of little value in the effort to understand why pilots were losing control. At the critical speeds just above and below the speed of sound, shock waves in the tunnel would choke off the airflow around the model."

Under the showers of the latter rain the inventions of man, the human machinery, will at times be swept away, the boundary of man's authority will be as broken reeds, and the Holy Spirit will speak through the living, human agent, with convincing power. No one then will watch to see if the sentences are well rounded off, if the grammar is faultless. The living water will flow in God's own channels. (White, *Selected Messages*, book 2, pp. 58–59)

It's not easy to fly when you're stuck on the ground. Much of our troubles might be avoided by keeping in contact with heaven, letting our prayers and thoughts ascend to the heavenly sanctuary, lifting us heavenward. Any hope for solving the speed barrier depended on being in the air. The laboratory had to be the sky.

Therefore, in Britain, a select group of pilots was asked to risk their lives to get the answers. One of them was Eric Brown, a member of a government high-speed test unit. His assignment was to deliberately fly a Spitfire into this dangerous region.

"Capt. Eric Brown: "Of course, when you're young and you're in a job like a research test pilot, you are very keen to try and beat this so-called barrier. There is always that feeling you have—a ridiculous feeling the young will have—of immortality. And I think this is what allows you to press on."

How blessed it is to know that immortality is more than a feeling!

"Capt. Eric Brown: I was certainly of the opinion that I was getting to my limit. There is always the risk that your muscles will not hold out in this situation, and you will relax your grip on the stick. And then, that will allow the aircraft, of course, to go steeper and steeper, with the end result probably fatal."

"Stacy Keach (Narrator): Another member of the team, Tony Martindale, barely survived a crash. The engine on his Spitfire exploded as he approached the speed of sound. Its propeller came off. He escaped with a broken back. Others weren't so lucky. Four of the six test pilots from the high-speed unit died at Farnborough doing these tests."

How could this go on? Well, it was a wartime measure and "…the risks and sacrifice helped reveal why these World War II fighter planes were going out of control."

"And I heard a voice from heaven saying unto me, Write, Blessed are the dead which die in the Lord from henceforth: Yea, saith the Spirit, that may rest from their labours; and their works do follow them" (Rev. 14:13).

"Greater love hath no man than this, that a man lay down his life for his friends" (John 15:13).

"Stacy Keach (Narrator): But on October 10th, the rocket motor behaved perfectly. Yeager reached 658 miles an hour. But at the edge of the barrier, he hit the very problem that had foiled everyone else."

"Brig. Gen. Chuck Yeager: When we got the airplane up to 94% of the speed of sound, and I'm sitting out there, and I decided to turn the airplane—I pulled back on the control column. Nothing happened. The airplane just went the way it was headed, and I said, 'Man, we've got a problem.' So, I raked the rockets off and jettisoned the liquid oxygen and alcohol, and came down and landed, and got the engineers together and we had a little heart-to-heart talk."

What God speaks to the saints individually comes to light as they commune with one another. "Then they that feared the LORD spake often one to another: and the LORD hearkened, and heard it, and a book of remembrance was written before him for them that feared the LORD, and that thought upon his name" (Mal. 3:16).

When Yeager and the staff did this, what happened? Yeager said, "We've got a problem, and because the airplane may pitch up or pitch down, I've lost the ability to control it."

"Stacy Keach (Narrator):…Fortunately, the engineers thought they had the answer: a new all-moving tail. Other planes could only move a small portion of the tail. On the X-1, the entire assembly could move. It hadn't been used before, but they thought it might stabilize the plane. First, it had to be checked out." The X-1 was airlifted by a B-29 bomber and released at a high altitude.

"Brig. Gen. Chuck Yeager: You're in a very dark hole under the B-29, and when you drop clear of the B-29, you're in bright sunlight. When I got above 94% of the speed of sound, the nose begins to come up on the airplane. I just cranked the leading edge up on the horizontal stabilizer [on the tail] to keep the nose down. When we went a little faster, the mach meter went off the scale and when it did, all the buffeting smoothed out, because the supersonic flow [shock waves] went over the whole airplane. And even I knew we had gotten above the speed of sound."

For the elect, the flexible tail section could perhaps be viewed as an inflexible, unrepentant pride of works and opinions, or maybe the tail section of the congregation, who have willing energies to unleash through union with God's Spirit providing a clear and present path of divine light (see Eph. 1:16–20). This, at heart, is what this book is all about.

Once passed the shock waves, there is no longer a problem with fixing the design because the shock waves are behind the craft. In other words, passed the barrier, the increase of power from above is followed by acceleration of the gospel on earth. The remnant, when flying beyond the barrier, will sound off the loud cry likened to the sonic boom that startles the earth. Even though pilots now routinely fly much faster than the speed of sound, they still return to the ground again, but the final landing of the Angel whose strong voice is heard worldwide will be upon none other than the sea of glass.

The aeronautical industry said that it was an impossible barrier—it couldn't be crossed. They called it the sonic wall. What happened to get a plane through the shock waves? There were a lot of design changes that got close, but only when the inflexible part was made moveable did success come.

> The church is God's agency for the proclamation of truth, empowered by Him to do a special work; and if she is loyal to Him, obedient to all His commandments, there will dwell within her the excellency of divine grace. If she will be true to her allegiance, if she will honor the Lord God of Israel, there is no power that can stand against her. (White, *The Acts of the Apostles*, p. 600)

Threshold Crossing Day

Wartime is what drove our test pilots and engineers to overcome apparently insurmountable, unseen counterforces. We as Christians are assured of victory in our unseen spiritual warfare against the fallen angels, world, and flesh by weapons furnished from heaven (see Eph. 6:10–18). "For though we walk in the flesh, we do not war after the flesh: (For the weapons of our warfare are not carnal, but mighty through God to the pulling down of strong holds;)" (2 Cor. 10:3, 4).

The surest word of prophecy (see 2 Peter 1:19) is undoubtedly a trusted weapon. "This charge I commit unto thee, son Timothy, according to the prophecies which went before on thee, that thou by them mightest war a good warfare" (1 Tim. 1:18).

Along with prophecy, we have prayer with thanksgiving (see Phil. 4:6) and perseverance of faith. "Rejoice evermore. Pray without ceasing. In every thing give thanks: for this is the will of God in Christ Jesus concerning you. Quench not the Spirit. Despise not prophesyings. Prove all things; hold fast that which is good" (1 Thess. 5:16–21). With such an armory, the elect is granted the privilege of accelerating the day of the Lord.

Accelerator 1—Hastening Prayers of the Elect

> *It is a delight for God to hear our prayers of faith, especially regarding obstacles thrown in our path while making efforts to do His will.*

It is a delight for God to hear our prayers of faith, especially regarding obstacles thrown in our path while making efforts to do His will. In Luke 18:1, Jesus provided the remedy for losing heart (faith) in moments of distress and temptation. The privilege of the saints who are accustomed to answered prayers is praying throughout the present window of opportunity, moving their congregations to repentance and revival ahead of the coming global crises, when it may be difficult to even attend church.

Revelation 8:3–4 reminds us of increased power through gatherings of the saints in united prayer in the end times. It is a source of sweetness to the Lord. "And another angel came and stood at the altar, having a golden censer; and there was given unto him much incense, that he should offer it with the prayers of all saints upon the golden altar which was before the throne. And the smoke of the incense, which came with the prayers of the saints, ascended up before God out of the angel's hand."

As far back as the later 1800s, it was time to ask for the latter rain. While the numbers of worshippers in churches generally continue to be strong over the years, is something perhaps amiss?

> "Ask ye of the Lord rain in the time of the latter rain." Do not rest satisfied that in the ordinary course of the season, rain will fall. Ask for it. The growth and perfection of the seed rests not with the husbandman. God alone can ripen the harvest. But <u>man's co-operation is required</u>. God's work for us demands the action of our mind, the exercise of our faith. We must seek His favors with the whole heart if the showers of grace are to come to us. We should improve every opportunity of placing ourselves in the channel of blessing. Christ has said, "Where two or three are gathered together in My name, there am I in the midst." The convocations of the church, as in camp meetings, the assemblies of the home church, and all occasions where there is personal labor for souls, are God's appointed opportunities for giving the early and the latter rain.
>
> But let none think that in attending these gatherings, their duty is done. A mere attendance upon all the meetings that are held will not in itself bring a blessing to the soul. It is not an immutable law that all who attend general gatherings

or local meetings shall receive large supplies from heaven. The circumstances may seem to be favorable for a rich outpouring of the showers of grace. But God Himself must command the rain to fall. Therefore we should not be remiss in supplication. We are not to trust to the ordinary working of providence. We must pray that God will unseal the fountain of the water of life. And we must ourselves receive of the living water. Let us, with contrite hearts, pray most earnestly that *now, in the time of the latter rain*, the showers of grace may fall upon us. At every meeting we attend our prayers should ascend, that *at this very time* God will impart warmth and moisture to our souls. As we seek God for the Holy Spirit, it will work in us meekness, humbleness of mind, a conscious dependence upon God for the perfecting latter rain. If we pray for the blessing in faith, we shall receive it as God has promised. (White, *Testimonies to Ministers and Gospel Workers*, p. 508, emphasis added)

James, after speaking of spiritual rains (see 5:7–9), continues with a natural follow-up in verse 16: "The effectual fervent prayer of a righteous man availeth much." Who is righteous? You and I are, when we daily take up the cross of coming to Jesus at the willing cost of all else. Have we devoted ourselves to Him today, not looking at our past works or sins? If we have confessed and repented, seeking forgiveness, then we are righteous in Christ and can pray prevailing prayers.

"O Israel, return unto the LORD thy God; for thou hast fallen by thine iniquity. Take with you words, and turn to the LORD: say unto him, Take away all iniquity, and receive us graciously" (Hosea 14:1, 2). If one righteous person avails much in fervent prayer, what would a network of righteous ones avail when praying for the ultimate theme? "Prepare ye the way of the Lord, make his paths straight....And all flesh shall see the salvation of God" (Luke 3:4, 6). Without hesitation, we are assured that the Lord will lose no time responding.

In a contest, what is the defense?—It's the side that functions to protect its turf; on the other hand, the offense goes for that turf. "And He went a little farther, and fell on His face, and prayed, saying, O my Father, if it be possible, let this cup pass from me: nevertheless not as I will but as Thou wilt" (Matt. 26:39). It was then that Jesus could stand to face a crowd bent on His destruction and eliminate the threat of not enduring to the end. He "went forth, and said unto them, Whom seek ye" (John 18:4)? Twice they fell back before Jesus permitted himself to be taken. This was the moment when the tide was turned in the controversy between good and evil.

What is the language of Scripture regarding the availing prayers of the elect? After telling the parable of the widow who received her justice from the unjust judge after wearying him with her continual pleas, Jesus added, "And shall not God avenge his own elect, which cry day and night unto him, though he bear long with them? I tell you that he will avenge them speedily. Nevertheless when the Son of man cometh, shall he find faith on the earth" (Luke 18:7, 8)? To rephrase that question, we might ask, "Is there any doubt about the Lord's desire to return within our generation?"

Along with the privilege of availing prayer, the elect are the voices of the three angels beginning faintly, then swelling into a loud cry from the outpouring of the Spirit and accompanied by new, prophetic light shining on the path before them.

> When the Third Angel's Message shall go forth with a loud voice, the whole earth shall be lightened with His glory, the Holy Spirit is poured out upon His people. The revenue of glory has been accumulating for this closing work of the Third Angel's Message. The prayers that have been ascending for the fulfillment of the promise, the descent of the Holy Spirit, *not*

one has been lost. Each prayer has been accumulating, ready to overflow and pour forth a healing flood of heavenly influence and *accumulated light* all over the world. (White, *Manuscript Releases*, vol. 1, pp. 180–181, emphasis added)

The presentation of this message is to result in the conversion and sanctification of souls. We are to feel the power of the Spirit of God in this movement. This is a wonderful, definite message; it means everything to the receiver, and it is to be proclaimed with a loud cry. We must have a true, abiding faith that this message will go forth with increasing importance till the close of time. (White, *Counsels on Diet and Foods*, pp. 36–37)

Next is a look at one individual's experience of availing prayer:

"Dr. K," I continued, "it is very important that you and I recognize the difficulty fencing you in on all sides, and that God alone can move those mountains out of the way and set you free. I have learned by experience that we should leave nothing to chance, but do everything possible to cooperate with God so that He can bring any conflict with the forces of evil to a glorious end. We want that outcome to exalt our great Redeemer before heaven and the rest of the universe.

"I will need your help with a few things. Do you have a pen and a sheet of paper handy so that you can take a few notes? I would like you to write me a letter outlining all the information you have given me today. There are two reasons for this. First, I want to present your letter before the Lord in a very special way as soon as I receive it. Also, I need to read it over every so often to deep all details fresh in my mind. That way I can keep my intercession sharp and meaningful." (Morneau, *When You Need Incredible Answers to Prayer*, pp. 41–42)

The often-surprising fact is that the Father's reason for inviting our prayers is that He loves to hear us, especially when it comes to problem solving. "Thou hast caused men to ride over our heads; we went through fire and through water: but thou broughtest us out into a wealthy place" (Ps. 66:12). Though the heaviest heat of Satan has been felt by the elect, their prevailing prayers will guarantee Satan's extermination, which he knows too well.

> "Sir, I believe that Satan and his spirit associates have for a long time been planning to bring distress, suffering, and anguish into your life, and, if the opportunity presented itself, to actually destroy you.
>
> "The main reason for such an attack is that you are a Seventh-day Adventist. Years ago a spirit worshiper told me that we are the people that Satan hates most on the face of the earth." (Morneau, *When You Need Incredible Answers to Prayer*, p. 40)

How is likeness to Christ's character linked to bringing Satan's opposition to nothing?

> "Jesus, when He had cried again with a loud voice, yielded up the ghost. And, behold, the veil of the temple was rent in twain from the top to the bottom; and the earth did quake, and the rocks rent; and the graves were opened; and many bodies of the saints which slept arose, and came out of the graves after his resurrection, and went into the holy city, and appeared unto many. Now when the centurion, and they that were with Him, watching Jesus, saw the earthquake, and those things that were done, they feared greatly, saying, Truly this was the Son of God" (Matt. 27:50–54).
>
> Every time that I read those five verses of Scripture it never fails that a cherished quotation from *The Desire of Ages* comes

to mind. "Love for God, zeal for His glory, and love for fallen humanity, brought Jesus to earth to suffer and to die. This was the controlling power of His life. This principle He bids us adopt" (p. 330).

As I became acquainted with these passages at the time I was first seeking a solid relationship with Christ, I made them a subject of prayer, and sought from God the Father those elements of righteousness and a character like that of Christ, I remember well how as the Spirit imparted to me Jesus' divine love for fallen humanity I found myself becoming deeply concerned with the well-being of others. That longing compelled me to begin praying with great earnestness that God's Holy Spirit would minister the graces of redemption to the subjects of my prayers.

It was also the time I started seeing my prayers answered in wonderful and exciting ways. As I said in the preface, since I wrote my last book on prayer the Lord has taken me from being a door opener and is now involving me in His work of moving mountains. And as I help individuals to acquire a solid relationship with Christ, their power-filled prayers also open the way for the Holy Spirit to move mountains out of the way of someone else's salvation.

I believe that in the earth made new those who in this present life involve themselves in the Lord's work of moving mountains will receive the greatest rewards. Every so often an angel of the Lord will introduce you to a person whose salvation will be traced back to your power-filled prayers. Prayers that opened the way for the Holy Spirit to accomplish mighty works of redemption in that individual's behalf. I can imagine how thrilled we will be when we meet such a person.

Sometime ago a minister who had read and enjoyed my books on prayer asked why I place so much importance on the scene at Calvary. "I know many good reasons that you might give me, but what stands above all others in your mind?"

Immediately I directed my thoughts to the Holy of Holies of the heavenly sanctuary, and silently said: "Dear Jesus, please help." Instantly the Spirit of God helped me to reply, "That's where the power is."

Yes, that's where we can find the power that will give us victory over self, sin, the allurement of the world, and, above all, over the power of the fallen angels. The power of God unto salvation (Rom. 1:16), it will enable us to eat of the tree of life in the midst of the paradise of God (Rev. 2:7), and make it possible for us to sit with Jesus on His throne (Rev. 3:21). It's the power of our Lord Jesus, our Strength and our Redeemer. That is why I try to inspire others to involve themselves in a prayer ministry that finds its power at the foot of the cross of Christ. (Morneau, *When You Need Incredible Answers to Prayer*, p. 29–31)

When the outcome of prayer is associated with sensing God's immediate presence, it expands territory for the kingdom of God in a manner that no other activity, however well thought out, discussed, or planned, could alone accomplish.

Accelerator 2—Faith Shaken, but Persevering

Can the hastening task of a majority elect be reached in our time? "For he will finish the work, and cut it short in righteousness: because a short work will the Lord make upon the earth" (Rom. 9:28). Evidently, something will shorten the delay and the path to the next-awaited sign—a spiritual majority which only God will recognize when it is fulfilled.

While the elect is praying for a majority, He allows a shaking of the Laodiceans outwardly and inwardly. "So then because thou art lukewarm, and neither cold nor hot, I will spue thee out of my mouth" (Rev. 3:16). They continue to be given opportunities to repent during the investigative judgment. The straight testimony to the Laodiceans declares the hidden intents of the heart. "For the word of God is quick, and powerful, and sharper than any twoedged sword, piercing even to the dividing asunder of soul and spirit, and of the joints and marrow, and is a discerner of the thoughts and intents of the heart" (Heb. 4:12).

> The Laodicean message applies to the people of God who profess to believe present truth. The greater part are lukewarm professors, having a name but no zeal. God signified that He wanted men at the great heart of the work to correct the state of things existing there and to stand like faithful sentinels at their post of duty. He has given them light at every point, to instruct, encourage, and confirm them, as the case required. But notwithstanding all this, those who should be faithful and true, fervent in Christian zeal, of gracious temper, knowing and loving Jesus earnestly, are found aiding the enemy to weaken and discourage those whom God is using to build up the work. The term "lukewarm" is applicable to this class. They profess to love the truth, yet are deficient in Christian fervor and devotion. They dare not give up wholly and run the risk of the unbeliever, yet they are unwilling to die to self and follow out closely the principles of their faith. (White, *Testimonies for the Church*, vol. 4, p. 87)

When the appeals of the Holy Spirit, prayers, and admonitions have been exhausted and the larger part of the remnant still remains lukewarm, then various faith crises are reluctantly permitted. The word "crisis" comes from the Greek *krisis*, meaning "decision," reflecting back to Joel

3:14: "Multitudes, multitudes in the valley of decision: for the day of the LORD is near in the valley of decision." A crisis is typically a moment of pressured decision under great duress.

Coinciding with the judgment message to the Laodiceans is a sharp deterioration of outward stability and security on the earth. Various calamities, horrific crimes, and economic and international uncertainty impart a sense of urgency that things can't go on like this for long. The lack of response of the church brethren in not heeding Christ's invitation is similar to that of society at large during the developing crisis—a shift toward social conformity instead of individual freedom to follow one's convictions. These outward pressures, combined with the shaking message of Revelation, compel remnant membership to either repent for being lukewarm or remain unmoved by heaven's invitations and thereby have no worthwhile reason to endure.

> *When the appeals of the Holy Spirit, prayers, and admonitions have been exhausted and the larger part of the remnant still remains lukewarm, then various faith crises are reluctantly permitted.*

> I was pointed to the providence of God among His people and was shown that every trial made by the refining, purifying process upon professed Christians proves some to be dross. The fine gold does not always appear. In every religious crisis some fall under temptation. The shaking of God blows away multitudes like dry leaves. Prosperity multiplies a mass of professors. Adversity purges them out of the church. As a class, their spirits are not steadfast with God. They go out from us because they are not of us; for when tribulation or persecution arises because of the word, many are offended. (White, *Testimonies for the Church*, vol. 4, p. 89)

The following passage represents the danger that faces the lukewarm in a time of approaching crisis. When God came to Mt. Sinai to meet with Moses and the congregation, His voice shook the earth. Now, from His antitypical sanctuary, where we meet Him by faith, God's voice shakes the earth and heaven.

> But ye are come unto mount Sion, and unto the city of the living God, the heavenly Jerusalem, and to an innumerable company of angels, To the general assembly and church of the firstborn, which are written in heaven, and to God the Judge of all, and to the spirits of just men made perfect, And to Jesus the mediator of the new covenant, and to the blood of sprinkling, that speaketh better things than that of Abel. See that ye refuse not him that speaketh. For if they escaped not who refused him that spake on earth, much more shall not we escape, if we turn away from him that speaketh from heaven: Whose voice then shook the earth: but now he hath promised, saying, Yet once more I shake not the earth only, but also heaven. And this word, Yet once more, signifieth the removing of those things that are shaken, as of things that are made, that those things which cannot be shaken may remain. Wherefore we receiving a kingdom which cannot be moved, let us have grace, whereby we may serve God acceptably with reverence and godly fear: For our God is a consuming fire. (Hebrews 12:22–29)

There is an elect within the remnant which remains (is not shaken out). Hebrews 13:1 appears to be a continuation of chapter 12: "Let brotherly love continue." Interestingly, the original Greek word for "continue" is the same as that for "remain" in Hebrews 12:27: "that those things which cannot be shaken may remain." In addition, the Greek for "brotherly love" is *philadelphia*. Therefore, in essence, Hebrews 13:1 is saying, "Let

Philadelphia remain." Thus, we can refer to the elect of the remnant as Philadelphia who remains after Laodicea has unfortunately been spewed out. In many of Jesus' parables is found this opposing duality within the church—wheat and the tares, good and bad fish, good and bad fruit, five wise and five foolish virgins, etc. "Because thou [Philadelphia] hast kept the word of my patience, I also will keep thee from the hour of temptation, which shall come upon all the world, to try them that dwell upon the earth" (Rev. 3:10).

The shaking, along with the minority elect's prayers, brings compelling conviction before fellow brethren in the form of a question posed by Moses, but modified for the last crisis: "Who is on the Lord's side for His imminent return?" Then enters the bad news and good news:

> Satan will work his miracles to deceive; he will set up his power as supreme. The church may appear as about to fall, but it does not fall. It remains, while the sinners in Zion will be sifted out—the chaff separated from the precious wheat. This is a terrible ordeal, but nevertheless it must take place. None but those who have been overcoming by the blood of the Lamb and the word of their testimony will be found with the loyal and true, without spot or stain of sin, without guile in their mouths. We must be divested of our self-righteousness and arrayed in the righteousness of Christ. (White, *Selected Messages*, book 2, p. 380)

By all appearances, the remnant will appear to be headed for elimination. The aftermath may well result in some form of reduction of the organization, but that assemblage, with many coming in, will constitute a majority elect and very likely even swell the ranks to surpass previous membership. This is why the enemies of the remnant become enraged; what they perceived as an apparent defeat only turned out to be a greater comeback than they possibly could have foreseen.

The contest is between the commandments of God and the commandments of men. In this time the gold will be separated from the dross in the church. True godliness will be clearly distinguished from the appearance and tinsel of it. Many a star that we have admired for its brilliancy will then go out in darkness. Chaff like a cloud will be borne away on the wind, even from places where we see only floors of rich wheat. All who assume the ornaments of the sanctuary, but are not clothed with Christ's righteousness, will appear in the shame of their own nakedness.

When trees without fruit are cut down as cumberers of the ground, when multitudes of false brethren are distinguished from the true, then the hidden ones will be revealed to view, and with hosannas range under the banner of Christ. Those who have been timid and self-distrustful will declare themselves openly for Christ and His truth. The most weak and hesitating in the church will be as David—willing to do and dare. The deeper the night for God's people, the more brilliant the stars. Satan will sorely harass the faithful; but, in the name of Jesus, they will come off more than conquerors. Then will the church of Christ appear "fair as the moon, clear as the sun, and terrible as an army with banners.

The seeds of truth that are being sown by missionary efforts will then spring up and blossom and bear fruit. Souls will receive the truth who will endure tribulation and praise God that they may suffer for Jesus. "In the world ye shall have tribulation: but be of good cheer; I have overcome the world." When the overflowing scourge shall pass through the earth, when the fan is purging Jehovah's floor, God will be the help of His people. The trophies of Satan may be exalted on high, but the faith of the pure and holy will not be daunted. (White, *Testimonies for the Church*, vol. 5, pp. 81–82)

Accelerator 3—Advancing Scripture Light

History repeats itself, and the same is true for spiritual history. The birth of Adventism was made possible by the small flock whose faith survived the Great Disappointment, and having been refined through the ordeal, they were blessed with advancing biblical guidance specific to their time—links of a golden chain of truth. Through united small group study and prayer, they opened the door for supping with Christ and gained divine favor and guidance through even dreams and visions. Therefore today, small groups may form to seek the guidance of advancing light from His Word.

What can take place through groups, small or large, embracing these accelerators for receiving the latter rain? Advancing light from God's Word accompanies rain revival, which was the case during the last window of opportunity in the late 1800s. Notice again the vital link between refined character and the reception of God's gift of guiding Bible light.

> When the latter rain comes upon the people of God, you must have a preparation to press right on, because those whose vessels are clean, whose hands are free just when that latter rain comes, *get the light that comes from on high*, and their voices are lifted, every one, to proclaim the commandments of God and the testimony of Jesus Christ. (White, *Sermons and Talks*, vol. 1, p. 50)

The outpouring of the second global rain causes the third angel's message to become a global loud cry. Jesus said that He is the light of the world. When that light shines brighter, more is discovered about Him (new gospel light unfolding throughout the ages), and His light goes on to reveal progressive end-time instruction. The light that shines with the second Pentecost is brighter gospel light and new prophetic light that build upon the old. On key occasions in spiritual history, this has been foundational to notable revivals. The stir that was created across Europe and spilled over to the new world during the Reformation was due to the Holy Spirit bringing advancing Scripture light.

Progressing prophetic light may be expected when the Lord sees a church of majority elect. New light given to an un-ripened congregation would probably result in the chaos of a variety of fanatical extremes. Considering that the results of new light can be expected to generate great interest, as well as controversy, it can only be given to a church with the humility and wisdom to receive it. Then the latter rain and accompanying light will fall with intensity.

"Great truths that have lain unheeded and unseen since the day of Pentecost, are to shine from God's word in their native purity. To those who truly love God the Holy Spirit will reveal truths that have faded from the mind, and will also reveal truths that are entirely new" (White 1987, p. 1651).

"Wouldn't it be strange if Jesus would give light to start us on our journey and then allow the light to shut off or fade out as we get into the darkest period of earth's history" (Frazee 2017, p. 52).

"Some passages are placed beyond the reach of human minds until such a time as God chooses, in His own wisdom, to open them" (White 1868, p. 377).

> Questions were asked at that time. "Sister White, do you think that the Lord has any new and increased light for us as a people?" I answered, "Most assuredly. I do not only think so, but can speak understandingly. I know that there is precious truth to be unfolded to us if we are the people that are to stand in the

day of God's preparation." (White, *Selected Messages*, book 3, p.174)

The following is a comment on Revelation 10, especially verses 3 and 4, which remain mysterious. This chapter is central to the theme of the final movements being covered here.

> The special light given to John which was expressed in the seven thunders was a delineation of events which would transpire under the first and second angels' messages. It was not best for the people to know these things, for their faith must necessarily be tested. In the order of God most wonderful and advanced truths would be proclaimed. The first and second angels' messages were to be proclaimed, but no further light was to be revealed before these messages had done their specific work. This is represented by the angel standing with one foot on the sea, proclaiming with a most solemn oath that time would be no longer [see Rev. 10].
>
> This time which the angel declares with a solemn oath, is not the end of this world's history, neither of probationary time, but of prophetic time, which should precede the advent of our Lord. That is, the people will not have another message upon definite time. After this period of time, reaching from 1842 to 1844, there can be no definite tracing of the prophetic time. The longest reckoning reaches to the autumn of 1844. (White, *Manuscript Releases*, vol. 1, p. 100)

We remain under the work and fulfillment of the first and second angels' messages since no one has yet received the mark of the beast, which constitutes the warning of third angel's message (see Rev. 14:9–11). The deadly wound of the papal beast of Revelation 13 is yet to be fully healed; thus, while the third angel's message is being proclaimed now, it is presented only as a warning of what is to come, but not yet as a fulfillment. Therefore, it appears that the mysteries of the seven thunders will be made known during developments in world affairs, which actually call for the warnings of the third angel's messages after the first and second have done their work—namely, the proclaiming of the pre-advent judgment and the fall of Babylon, the apostate churches (see Rev.14:6–8).

> In every age there is a new development of truth, a message of God to the people of that generation. The old truths are all essential; new truth is not independent of the old, but an unfolding of it....
>
> ...Truth in Christ and through Christ is measureless. The student of Scripture looks, as it were, into a fountain that deepens and broadens as he gazes into its depths. Not in this life shall we comprehend the mystery of God's love in giving His Son to be the propitiation for our sins. The work of our Redeemer on this earth is and ever will be a subject that will put to the stretch our highest imagination. Man may tax every mental power in the endeavor to fathom this mystery, but his mind will become faint and weary. The most diligent searcher will see before him a boundless, shoreless sea.
>
> The truth as it is in Jesus can be experienced, but never explained. Its height and breadth and depth pass our knowledge. We may task our imagination to the utmost, and then we shall see only dimly the outlines of a love that is unexplainable, that is as high as heaven, but that stooped to the earth to stamp the image of God on all mankind....
>
> ...Our life is to be bound up with the life of Christ; we are to draw constantly from Him, partaking of Him, the living Bread that came down from heaven, drawing from a fountain ever fresh, ever giving forth its abundant treasures. If we keep the Lord ever before us, allowing our hearts to go out

in thanksgiving and praise to Him, we shall have a continual freshness in our religious life. Our prayers will take the form of a conversation with God as we would talk with a friend. He will speak His mysteries to us personally. Often there will come to us a sweet joyful sense of the presence of Jesus. Often our hearts will burn within us as He draws nigh to commune with us as He did with Enoch. When this is in truth the experience of the Christian, there is seen in his life a simplicity, a humility, meekness, and lowliness of heart, that show to all with whom he associates that he has been with Jesus and learned of Him....

...When we eat Christ's flesh and drink His blood, the element of eternal life will be found in the ministry. There will not be a fund of stale, oft-repeated ideas. The tame, dull sermonizing will cease. The old truths will be presented, but they will be seen in a new light. There will be a new perception of truth, a clearness and a power that all will discern. Those who have the privilege of sitting under such a ministry will, if susceptible to the Holy Spirit's influence, feel the energizing power of a new life. The fire of God's love will be kindled within them. Their perceptive faculties will be quickened to discern the beauty and majesty of truth.

The faithful householder represents what every teacher of the children and youth should be. If he makes the word of God his treasure, he will continually bring forth new beauty and new truth....

...God's holy, educating Spirit is in His word. A light, a new and precious light, shines forth from every page. Truth is there revealed, and words and sentences are made bright and appropriate for the occasion, as the voice of God speaking to the soul.

The Holy Spirit loves to address the youth, and to discover to them the treasures and beauties of God's word. The promises spoken by the great Teacher will captivate the senses and animate the soul with spiritual power that is divine. There will grow in the fruitful mind a familiarity with divine things that will be as a barricade against temptation....

...The significance of the Jewish economy is not yet fully comprehended. Truths vast and profound are shadowed forth in its rites and symbols. The gospel is the key that unlocks its mysteries. Through a knowledge of the plan of redemption, its truths are opened to the understanding. Far more than we do, it is our privilege to understand these wonderful themes. We are to comprehend the deep things of God. Angels desire to look into the truths that are revealed to the people who with contrite hearts are searching the word of God, and praying for greater lengths and breadths and depths and heights of the knowledge which He alone can give.

As we near the close of this world's history, the prophecies relating to the last days especially demand our study. The last book of the New Testament scriptures is full of truth that we need to understand. (White, *Christ's Object Lessons*, pp. 127–133)

Opposition Awakens

A group of bike riders crossing a mountain pass on the uphill side labor and sweat, moving at a crawl; but they press on with the downhill ride in mind. That's when gravity basically does all the work, plus a little brake action. After decades of uphill occupying until He comes, the flock presses on until passing through a gate at the top where they are sealed with the name of the Father in their foreheads (see Rev. 7:3). From there, it is a downhill ride when the Holy Spirit basically does the work through human vessels, moving their generation to the finish line. The greatest obstacle, therefore, lies in wait at the top. What might be expected as we come to the crest of the mountain? "As we approach the close of time, as the people of God stand upon the borders of the heavenly Canaan, Satan will, as of old, redouble his efforts to prevent them from entering the goodly land. He lays his snares for every soul" (White 1890, p. 457).

Since persecution largely ended in the west after the dark ages, our world has more or less tolerated coexistence with God's people. Is Satan's oppressive power limited only to nations where Christians are still forced underground by religious or atheistic authority? Is our longstanding freedom from religious persecution guaranteed never to change, with Satan giving up on trying to impose tyranny on the free world?

> The apostle Paul declares that "all that will live godly in Christ Jesus shall suffer persecution." [2 Timothy 3:12.] Why is it, then, that persecution seems in a great degree to slumber?—The only reason is, that the church has conformed to the world's standard, and therefore awakens no opposition. The religion which is current in our day is not of the pure and holy character that marked the Christian faith in the days of Christ and His apostles. It is only because of the spirit of compromise with sin, because the great truths of the Word of God are so indifferently regarded, because there is so little vital godliness in the church, that Christianity is apparently so popular with the world. Let there be a revival of the faith and power of the early church, and the spirit of persecution will be revived, and the fires of persecution will be rekindled. (White, *The Great Controversy*, p. 48)

Opposition arises as Satan's hosts attempt to thwart the coming revival and outpouring by convincing the unwitting masses that the flourishing movement of the advent hope is a threat to the common peace. His flocks are ensnared through his powerful arsenal of spiritual counterfeiting, vain traditions, the lure of lifestyle, and neglect or twisting of Scripture. Satan knows the door's location and importance. His armies are stationed to conduct the utmost warfare as we reach for the door where it will be raining on the other side.

> Many, both of ministers and people, will gladly accept those great truths which God has caused to be proclaimed at this time to prepare a people for the Lord's second coming. *The enemy of souls desires to hinder this work; and before the time for such a movement shall come, he will endeavor to prevent it by introducing a counterfeit.* In those churches which he can bring under his deceptive power he will make it appear that God's special blessing is poured out; there will be manifest what is thought to be great religious interest. Multitudes will exult that God is working marvelously for them, when the work is that of another spirit. Under a religious guise, Satan will seek to extend his influence over the Christian world. (White, *The Great Controversy*, p. 464, emphasis added)

The development of this counterfeit movement has been unfolding for some time now. The charismatic movement has crossed all denominational lines and even received official endorsement from the Roman Church. Through belief in the immortal soul, the charismatic movement has opened the door for spiritualism.

> Satan does all he can to keep souls from Christ. He was once an honored angel in heaven, and although he has lost his holiness, he has not lost his power. He exerts his power with terrible effect. He does not wait for his prey to come to him. He hunts for it. He goes to and fro in the earth like a roaring lion, seeking whom he may devour. He does not always wear the ferocious look of the lion, but when he can work to better effect

he transforms himself into an angel of light. He can readily exchange the roar of the lion for the most persuasive arguments or for the softest whisper. He has legions of angels to aid him in his work. He often conceals his snares, and allures by pleasing deception. He charms and deludes many by flattering their vanity. Through his agents he presents the pleasures of the world in an attractive light, and strews the path to hell with tempting flowers, and thus souls are charmed and ruined. (White, *Testimonies for the Church*, vol. 2, p. 287)

Popular Opposition Intensifies

The agencies of evil are combining their forces and consolidating. They are strengthening for the last great crisis. (White, *Testimonies for the Church*, vol. 9, p. 11)

As the opposition rises to a fiercer height, the servants of God are again perplexed; for it seems to them that they have brought the crisis. But conscience and the word of God assure them that their course is right; and although the trials continue, they are strengthened to bear them. The contest grows closer and sharper, but their faith and courage rise with the emergency. Their testimony is: "We dare not tamper with God's word, dividing His holy law; calling one portion essential and another nonessential, to gain the favor of the world. The Lord whom we serve is able to deliver us. Christ has conquered the powers of earth; and shall we be afraid of a world already conquered?" (White, *The Great Controversy*, p. 610)

"The commencement of that time of trouble"…does not refer to the time when the plagues shall begin to be poured out, but to a short period just before they are poured out, while Christ is in the sanctuary. At that time, while the work of salvation is closing, trouble will be coming on the earth, and the nations will be angry, yet held in check so as not to prevent the work of the third angel. At that time the "latter rain," or refreshing from the presence of the Lord, will come... (White, *Early Writings*, p. 85–86)

The phrase "nations will be angry" is taken from the seventh trumpet of Revelation 11:18, which portrays the closing of the pre-advent judgment. The above quote shows the link between the closing judgment/salvation work with that time when the latter rain may be expected. "Ask ye of the LORD rain in the time of the latter rain" (Zech. 10:1). Perhaps no better scenario can be found to match this lesser "time of trouble" than today when a couple of small, angry nations in another hemisphere can become a grave concern to the superpowers. "Christians should be preparing for what is soon to break upon the world as an overwhelming surprise, and this preparation they should make by diligently studying the word of God and striving to conform their lives to its precepts....God calls for a revival and a reformation" (White 1917, p. 626). This revival and reformation array His wife in righteousness (see Rev. 19:8). Revival and reformation, when it comes to pass, evokes from the adversary the "overwhelming surprise."

Barrier Crossing Assurance

"Keep in the channel of light, for there is to be more direct communication from heaven to earth" (White 1990, p. 310).

There will be messages of accusation against the people of God, similar to the work done by Satan in accusing God's people, and these messages will be sounding at the very time when

God is saying to His people, "Arise, shine; for thy light is come, and the glory of the LORD is risen upon thee. For, behold, the darkness shall cover the earth, and gross darkness the people: but the Lord shall arise upon thee, and His glory shall be seen upon thee." (White, *Testimonies to Ministers and Gospel Workers*, p. 42)

It is then that the Lord will intervene for His people, sending His Spirit's outpouring.

So shall they fear the name of the LORD from the west, and his glory from the rising of the sun. When the enemy shall come in like a flood, the Spirit of the LORD shall lift up a standard against him. And the Redeemer shall come to Zion, and unto them that turn from transgression in Jacob, saith the LORD [a sanctified congregation]. As for me, this is my covenant with them, saith the LORD; My spirit that is upon thee, and my words which I have put in thy mouth, shall not depart out of thy mouth, nor out of the mouth of thy seed, nor out of the mouth of thy seed's seed, saith the LORD, from henceforth and for ever [clear, continual communication from heaven]. (Isaiah 59:19–21)

A blessed day awaits His people as He carries them across the threshold of finishing their mission. In contrast, the world will be at its worst in that day, but "where sin abounded, grace did much more abound" (Rom. 5:20). The battle accelerates as the conditions come together. As the church approaches a united front, which is the barrier crossing or event horizon, we could say, then spiritual resistance becomes open accusation and persecution follows, after the door of outpouring is passed. As at the first Pentecost, the threat of open destruction awaits Christ's people after the border crossing of the second Pentecost, but this will only aid the gathering momentum. Pharaoh's next decree of threatening the lives of the Israelites was followed by their liberation seven days later.

Chapter 8

Passing Through the Banquet Door, No Turning Back

"Great changes are soon to take place in our world, and the final movements will be rapid ones" (White 1909, p. 11). These great changes take place with the release of the latter rain as the wise virgins enter the door of the wedding and carry invitations to the remaining populations of earth for the Tabernacles harvest.

> If all who claim to believe the truth for this time would use in His service the power that God has provided for them through Jesus Christ, we should see the working of the Spirit of God that would produce great changes. The divine blessing would be greatly increased by the cooperation of human agencies to communicate these blessings to the world. (White, *Manuscript Releases*, p. 461)

Although there is no time or sign given before the seal and latter rain begins falling from heaven, what are evidences to show that they have arrived? The following are a few of the changes that may be expected?

Greatest Spiritual Awakening of All Time

"The outpouring of the Spirit in apostolic days was the 'former rain,' and glorious was the result. But the 'latter rain' will be more abundant" (White 1898, p. 827). The loud cry of the third angel has already begun, but its full global strength is realized during Feast-of-Tabernacles outpouring. "[T]he loud cry of the third angel has already begun in the revelation of the righteousness of Christ…This is the beginning of the light of the angel whose glory shall fill the whole earth" (White 1958, p. 363).

> The power which stirred the people so mightily in the 1844 movement will again be revealed. The third angel's message will go forth, not in whispered tones, but with a loud voice.…
>
> …During the loud cry, the church, aided by the providential interpositions of her exalted Lord, will diffuse the knowledge of salvation so abundantly that light will be communicated to every city and town. The earth will be filled with the knowledge of salvation. So abundantly will the renewing Spirit of God have crowned with success the intensely active agencies, that the light of present truth will be seen flashing everywhere. (White, *Evangelism*, pp. 693–694)

Corresponding with the abundance of crowning success from God will be a significant shift in the current response to and support of gospel outreach.

> The treasury of the Lord is wanting funds with which to carry the work as fast as it is the pleasure of the Lord that it should go; and the world, seeing the indifference manifested, is not affected by the message as it would be if every heart were warm with the love, which in every act and word expresses its devotion as did the life of Christ, our Pattern.… The work then, must be observed of all nations, whether it is in an indifferent state, or moving in the fullness of the power of God. *When it*

reaches that stage that God's people walk with Him in such confidence as this chapter describes, the message will be attended by the refreshing showers of the latter rain, and the earth will be speedily lighted by His glory. (White, *Bible Training School*, November 1, 1911, par. 3, 4, emphasis added)

As we near the end, the gospel will go with greater and yet greater rapidity. And opportunities will be given us to give more and more of the means of which the Lord had made us His stewards. In this God would have us act as His colaborers. What a blessing, to be a worker and an heir with the world's Redeemer! If we suffer with Him, the promise is, we shall also reign with Him. As we hear the calls and demands being more and more urgently made for means to enter the many doors that are opening, we may know that the Lord's coming is nearing. Who would delay it by withholding for selfish gratification the means God has placed in our hands for this very work? (White, *Pacific Union Recorder*, Oct. 24, 1901, par. 13)

How may His people know that they have arrived at that point of communion faith/righteousness and thus the second Pentecost? "And ye shall know that I am in the midst of Israel, and that I am the LORD your God, and none else: and my people shall never be ashamed. And it shall come to pass *afterward*, that I will pour out my spirit upon all flesh; and your sons and your daughters shall prophesy, your old men shall dream dreams, your young men shall see visions" (Joel 2:27, 28, emphasis added). The effect upon the people giving the gospel is that the gifts of the Holy Spirit are fully activated (see Eph. 4:8–13), especially the supernatural gift of prophecy (verses 28, 29) to the extent that the prophesying is heard in mainstream conversation.

"Now we seem to be unnoticed, but this will not always be. Movements are at work to bring us to the front, and if our theories of truth can be picked to pieces by historians or the world's greatest men, it will be done"

(White 1946, p. 69). The fact that it will be impossible to pick our theories to pieces is, to a large extent, what ushers the truth into the public arena. The effect upon the hearers is deep-seated conviction resulting in compelling responses, either to receive the message or take up warfare against the messengers. This should not be a surprise since there hasn't been a change or evolution in human nature.

Inflow of Thousands for the Harvest

Outward evidence of rain is a massive inflow of new believers largely unfazed by the progression of persecution. From the last generation, a multitude which cannot be numbered will take their stand for the Way, the Truth, and the Life (see Rev. 7:9; Zech. 8:20–23; also the "Tabernacles of Revelation" subsection in chapter 4).

> And the Gentiles shall come to thy light, and kings to the brightness of thy rising. Lift up thine eyes round about, and see: all they gather themselves together, they come to thee: thy sons shall come from far, and thy daughters shall be nursed at thy side. Then thou shalt see, and flow together, and thine heart shall fear, and be enlarged; because the abundance of the sea shall be converted unto thee, the forces of the Gentiles shall come unto thee. (Isaiah 60:3–5)

Passing through the threshold of unlimited spiritual power, a sudden surge of incoming believers is expected. Many leave the fallen churches (see Rev. 18:4). Ministers and laity, in the power of the spirit of Elijah, will move great numbers to repentance and union with the remnant people.

> *Passing through the threshold of unlimited spiritual power, a sudden surge of incoming believers is expected.*

Christ used the wind as a symbol of the Spirit of God. As the wind bloweth whither it listeth, and we cannot tell whence it cometh or whither it goeth, so it is with the Spirit of God. We do not know through whom it will be manifested. But I speak not my own words when I say that God's Spirit will pass by those who have had their day of test and opportunity, but who have not *distinguished the voice of God* or appreciated the movings of His Spirit. Then thousands in the eleventh hour will see and acknowledge the truth. "Behold, the days come, saith the Lord, that the plowman shall overtake the reaper, and the treader of grapes him that soweth seed" (Amos 9:13). These *conversions to truth will be made with a rapidity that will surprise the church, and God's name alone will be glorified*. (White, *Manuscript Releases*, vol. 1, p. 179, emphasis added)

Many have let the gospel invitation go unheeded; they have been tested and tried; but mountainous obstacles have seemed to loom up before their faces, blocking their onward march. Through faith, perseverance, and courage, many will surmount these obstructions and walk out into the glorious light.

Almost unconsciously barriers have been erected in the strait and narrow way; stones of stumbling have been placed in the path; these will be rolled away. The safeguards which false shepherds have thrown around their flocks will become as nought; thousands will step out into the light, and work to spread the light. Heavenly intelligences will combine with the human agencies. Thus encouraged, the church will indeed arise and shine, throwing all her sanctified energies into the contest; thus the design of God is accomplished; the lost pearls are recovered. (White, *Evangelism*, pp. 692–693)

Before the final visitation of God's judgments upon the earth there will be among the people of the Lord such a revival of primitive godliness as has not been witnessed since apostolic times. [Then with this goal satisfied, comes the promise…] The Spirit and power of God will be poured out upon His children. At that time many will separate themselves from those churches in which the love of this world has supplanted love for God and His word. Many, both of ministers and people, will gladly accept those great truths which God has caused to be proclaimed at this time to prepare a people for the Lord's second coming. (White, *The Great Controversy*, p. 464)

"Notwithstanding the agencies combined against the truth, a large number take their stand upon the Lord's side" (White 1911, p. 612).

"The time is coming when there will be as many converted in a day as there were on the day of Pentecost, after the disciples had received the Holy Spirit" (White 1946, p. 692). Acts 2:41 records that on the day of Pentecost, three thousand souls were converted. This was the response given by one city; the last Pentecost will gain a similar response from cities around the earth.

"God will soon do great things for us, if we lie humble and believing at His feet.…More than one thousand will soon be converted in one day, most of whom will trace their first convictions to the reading of our publications" (White 1946, p. 693).

Great Changes in God's People

Thus the message of the third angel will be proclaimed. As the time comes for it to be given with greatest power, the Lord will work through humble instruments, leading the minds of those who consecrate themselves to His service. The laborers will be qualified rather by the unction of His Spirit than by the training of literary institutions. Men of faith and prayer will be constrained to go forth with holy zeal, declaring the words which God gives them. (White, *The Great Controversy*, p. 606)

God can breathe new life into every soul that sincerely desires to serve him, and can touch the lips with a live coal from off the altar, and cause them to become eloquent with his praise. Thousands of voices will be imbued with the power to speak forth the wonderful truths of God's word. The stammering tongue will be unloosed, and the timid will be made strong to bear courageous testimony to the truth. May the Lord help his people to *cleanse the soul temple* from every defilement, and to *maintain such a close connection with him* that they may be partakers of the *latter rain* when it shall be poured out. (White, *Gospel Workers*, p. 383, emphasis added)

The end of that last quote encapsulates a familiar, three-part sequence: 1) repentance and revival for sin cleansing, 2) communion righteousness, and 3) refreshing of rain, all within reach today.

I heard those clothed with the armor speak forth the truth with great power. It had effect. Many had been bound; some wives by their husbands, and some children by their parents. The honest who had been prevented from hearing the truth now eagerly laid hold upon it. All fear of their relatives was gone, and the truth alone was exalted to them. They had been hungering and thirsting for truth; it was dearer and more precious than life. I asked what had made this great change. An angel answered, "It is the latter rain, the refreshing from the presence of the Lord, the loud cry of the third angel." (White, *Early Writings*, p. 271)

Unrestrained Proclaiming of the Fall of Babylon

By the preaching, teaching, and prophesying through personal contact, meetings, media, and churches is heard the genuine revelation of Jesus Christ in clear contrast to the modern-day, ecumenical tower of Babylon.

> "I saw another angel come down from heaven, having great power; and the earth was lightened with his glory. And he cried mightily with a strong voice, saying, Babylon the great is fallen, is fallen, and is become the habitation of devils, and the hold of every foul spirit, and a cage of every unclean and hateful bird." "And I heard another voice from heaven, saying, Come out of her, My people, that ye be not partakers of her sins, and that ye receive not of her plagues." Revelation 18:1, 2, 4. (White, *The Great Controversy*, p. 603)

During the Tabernacles outpouring, the impact that the loud cry makes is the global-scale illumination of the stark contrast between the pride of Babylon, with her confusion of the gospel, and the infinite humility of Christ, whose same character is imparted to His people—the mystery of the gospel. "To whom God would make known what is the riches of the glory of this mystery among the Gentiles; which is Christ in you, the hope of glory" (Col. 1:27).

Unrepentant members of Babylon increasingly become like their leader, as the members of the elect become more like their Leader. The loud cry swells this contrast of light and darkness until the appearing of Jesus. "But if our gospel be hid, it is hid to them that are lost: In whom the god of this world hath blinded the minds of them which believe not, lest the light of the glorious gospel of Christ, who is the image of God, should shine unto them" (2 Cor. 4:3, 4).

The prophet says, "I saw another angel come down from heaven, having great power; and the earth was lightened with his glory. And he cried mightily with a strong voice, saying, Babylon the great is fallen, is fallen, and is become the habitation of devils" (Revelation 18:1, 2). This is the same message that was given by the second angel. Babylon is fallen, "because she made all nations drink of the wine of the wrath of her fornication" (Revelation 14:8). What is that wine?—Her false doctrines. She has given to the world a false sabbath instead of the Sabbath of the fourth commandment, and has repeated the falsehood that Satan first told Eve in Eden—the natural immortality of the soul. Many kindred errors she has spread far and wide, "teaching for doctrines the commandments of men" (Matthew 15:9). (White, *Selected Messages*, book 2, p. 118)

The sins of Babylon will be laid open. The fearful results of enforcing the observances of the church by civil authority, the inroads of spiritualism, the stealthy but rapid progress of the papal power—all will be unmasked. By these solemn warnings the people will be stirred. Thousands upon thousands will listen who have never heard words like these. (White, *The Great Controversy*, p. 606)

The Sabbath will be the great test of loyalty, for it is the point of truth especially controverted. When the final test shall be brought to bear upon men, then the line of distinction will be drawn between those who serve God and those who serve Him not. While the observance of the false sabbath in compliance with the law of the state, contrary to the fourth commandment, will be an avowal of allegiance to a power that is in opposition to God, the keeping of the true Sabbath, in obedience to God's law, is an evidence of loyalty to the Creator. While one class, by accepting the sign of submission to earthly powers, receive the mark of the beast, the other choosing the token of allegiance to divine authority, receive the seal of God. (White, *The Great Controversy*, p. 605)

The Value of Miracles, Signs, and Wonders

Servants of God, with their faces lighted up and shining with holy consecration, will hasten from place to place to proclaim the message from heaven. By thousands of voices, all over the earth, the warning will be given. Miracles will be wrought, the sick will be healed, and signs and wonders will follow the believers. Satan also works, with lying wonders, even bringing down fire from heaven in the sight of men. Revelation 13:13. Thus the inhabitants of the earth will be brought to take their stand. (White, *The Great Controversy*, p. 612)

Though not lacking in miracles, the real test of the Lord's side will be the authority of His Holy Word, with emphasis on the faith of Jesus and the Ten Commandments (see Rev. 14:12).

> *Though not lacking in miracles, the real test of the Lord's side will be the authority of His Holy Word, with emphasis on the faith of Jesus and the Ten Commandments.*

It is impossible to give any idea of the experience of the people of God who shall be alive upon the earth when celestial glory and a repetition of the persecutions of the past are blended. They will walk in the light proceeding from the throne of God. By means of the angels there will be constant communication between heaven and earth. And

Satan, surrounded by evil angels, and claiming to be God, will work miracles of all kinds, to deceive, if possible, the very elect. God's people will not find their safety in working miracles, for Satan will counterfeit the miracles that will be wrought. God's tried and tested people will find their power in the sign spoken of in Exodus 31:12–18. They are to take their stand on the living word: "It is written." This is the only foundation upon which they can stand securely. Those who have broken their covenant with God will in that day be without God and without hope. (White, *Testimonies for the Church*, vol. 9, p. 16; at this time, no rain received means no sealing)

Open Persecution

During the latter rain, opposition turns from accusation to open persecution as multitudes from the nations are filling God's house.

> When the storm of persecution really breaks upon us, the true sheep will hear the true Shepherd's voice. Self-denying efforts will be put forth to save the lost, and many who have strayed from the fold will come back to follow the great Shepherd. The people of God will draw together, and present to the enemy a united front.... The love of Christ, the love of our brethren, will testify to the world that we have been with Jesus and learned of Him. Then will the message of the third angel swell to a loud cry, and the whole earth will be lightened with the glory of the Lord. (White, *Evangelism*, p. 693)

> As the people go to their former teachers with the eager inquiry, Are these things so? the ministers present fables, prophesy smooth things, to soothe their fears and quiet the awakened

Passing Through the Banquet Door, No Turning Back

> conscience. But since many refuse to be satisfied with the mere authority of men and demand a plain "Thus saith the Lord," the popular ministry, like the Pharisees of old, filled with anger as their authority is questioned, will denounce the message as of Satan and stir up the sin-loving multitudes to revile and persecute those who proclaim it. (White, *The Great Controversy*, p. 606)

Until now, there have been few obvious signs that Sunday persecution is on the horizon, except for Sunday blue laws, which at worse have been little more than inconvenience laws. The following also indicates that the latter rain (power attending the message) precipitates Sunday-law enforcement.

> As the controversy extends into new fields and the minds of the people are called to God's downtrodden law, Satan is astir. The <u>power</u> attending the message will only madden those who oppose it. The clergy will put forth almost superhuman efforts to shut away the light lest it should shine upon their flocks. By every means at their command they will endeavor to suppress the discussion of these vital questions. The church appeals to the strong arm of civil power, and, in this work, papists and Protestants unite. As the movement for Sunday enforcement becomes more bold and decided, the law will be invoked against commandment keepers. They will be threatened with fines and imprisonment, and some will be offered positions of influence, and other rewards and advantages, as inducements to renounce their faith. But their steadfast answer is: "Show us from the word of God our error"—the same plea that was made by Luther under similar circumstances. Those who are arraigned before the courts make a strong vindication of the truth, and some who hear them are led to take their stand to

keep all the commandments of God. Thus light will be brought before thousands who otherwise would know nothing of these truths. (White, *The Great Controversy*, p. 607)

With every rejection of truth the minds of the people will become darker, their hearts more stubborn, until they are entrenched in an infidel hardihood. In defiance of the warnings which God has given, they will continue to trample upon one of the precepts of the Decalogue, until they are led to persecute those who hold it sacred. Christ is set at nought in the contempt placed upon His word and His people. As the teachings of spiritualism are accepted by the churches, the restraint imposed upon the carnal heart is removed, and the profession of religion will become a cloak to conceal the basest iniquity. A belief in spiritual manifestations opens the door to seducing spirits and doctrines of devils, and thus the influence of evil angels will be felt in the churches. (White, *The Great Controversy*, p. 603)

Spiritual opposition develops into religious persecution, using the arm of the state (turbulence) during the "sound-barrier crossing," and escalates into the Battle of Armageddon (time of trouble of Dan. 12:1). However, like the Red Sea passage, floods were on both sides, yet the children of God made it across on dry ground. Though distressed, the saints are upheld by their acquired sense of His presence and promises, whereby they possess assurance that the walls of destruction will be held back from falling upon them. Relating to the flight allegory, perilous shock waves await this crossing. When general church rain revival appears imminent, Satan's forces evoke popular animosity that boils into open persecution, leading to his weapons of mass destruction—the move to global Sunday laws that will ultimately demand the lives of the noncompliant (see Rev. 13:3–5).

Abrupt Turnover

"For, behold, the day cometh, that shall burn as an oven; and all the proud, yea, and all that do wickedly, shall be stubble: and the day that cometh shall burn them up, saith the Lord of hosts, that it shall leave them neither root nor branch. But unto you that fear My name shall the Sun of Righteousness arise with healing in His wings; and ye shall go forth and grow up as calves of the stall" (Malachi 4:1, 2).

Here are brought plainly to view those who will be vessels unto honor; for they will receive the latter rain. Every soul who in the light now shining upon our pathway continues in sin will be blinded, and will accept the delusions that come from Satan. We are now nearing the close of this earth's history. Where are the faithful watchmen on the walls of Zion who will not slumber, but faithfully declare the time of night? (White, *Manuscript Releases*, vol. 1, p. 176)

Some had been shaken out and left by the way. The careless and indifferent, who did not join with those who prized victory and salvation enough to perseveringly plead and agonize for it, did not obtain it, and they were left behind in darkness, and their places were immediately filled by others taking hold of the truth and coming into the ranks.

The broken ranks will be filled up by those represented by Christ as coming in at the eleventh hour. There are many with whom the Spirit of God is striving. The time of God's destructive judgments is the time of mercy for those who [now] have no opportunity to learn what is truth. Tenderly will the Lord look upon them. His heart of mercy is touched, His hand is still stretched out to save, while the door is closed to those who would not enter. Large numbers will be admitted who in these last days hear the truth for the first time.

Standard after standard was left to trail in the dust as company after company from the Lord's army joined the foe and tribe after tribe from the ranks of the enemy united with the commandment-keeping people of God. (White, *Last Day Events*, p. 182)

When the Lord has determined that it is time for the seal and latter rain, the probation of the existing church closes in one unseen moment. Then pressed in with the crisis, the unsealed will not see the coming persecution as faith-confirming, but as a source of yielding their faith in order to secure life and provisions (see Rev. 13:17).

As the storm approaches, a large class who have professed faith in the third angel's message, but have not been sanctified through obedience to the truth, abandon their position and join the ranks of the opposition. By uniting with the world and partaking of its spirit, they have come to view matters in nearly the same light; and when the test is brought, they are prepared to choose the easy, popular side. Men of talent and pleasing address, who once rejoiced in the truth, employ their powers to deceive and mislead souls. They become the most bitter enemies of their former brethren. When Sabbathkeepers are brought before the courts to answer for their faith, these apostates are the most efficient agents of Satan to misrepresent and accuse them, and by false reports and insinuations to stir up the rulers against them. (White, *The Great Controversy*, p. 608)

Closing Time—Scanning the Eastern Sky

When the gospel has finished spreading and people cannot change which side they are on, the remaining earthly events are of a fixed duration, not to be altered; nevertheless, they come rather quickly. "Therefore shall her plagues come in one day" (Rev. 18:8; one year in prophetic time).

> I was pointed down to the time when the third angel's message was closing. The power of God had rested upon His people; they had accomplished their work and were prepared for the trying hour before them. They had received the latter rain, or refreshing from the presence of the Lord, and the living testimony had been revived. The last great warning had sounded everywhere, and it had stirred up and enraged the inhabitants of the earth who would not receive the message. (White, *Early Writings*, p. 279)

"They are threatened with destruction. The enthusiasm which animated them is gone; yet they cannot turn back. Then, feeling their utter helplessness, they flee to the Mighty One for strength" (White 1911, p. 608). They remember that for this occasion, Jesus imparted these words: "look up, and lift up your heads; for your redemption draweth nigh" (Luke 21:28). They begin to gaze toward the eastern sky and listen for the "trump of God." They continue returning to the clearing until faith becomes sight (see 1 Peter 1:8, 9).

Conclusion

All the signs important for closing the chapter of fallen earth are in place. The next sign is internal. When a majority, during today's window, takes hold of communion-level faith and cleansing repentance through the daily small rains, then God will have the delight of not holding back this time around. Then the captives of earth will suffer no further postponements.

Statistics show continuing growth, but how does this compare with global population expansion? As the work of beholding Christ to the level of hearing His voice in daily life overtakes the allure of external works, then statistical data can be set aside. Thus far the church has faced a barrier from earth's attractions, distractions, and unrelenting cares, leaving scarcely any space for God's small voice (see 1 Kings 19:11, 12). Today's issues of the great controversy surround an ecclesiastical and individual demonstration with a living visual aid—the life of godliness in a godless world, born out of soul-searching faith and repentance.

> Therefore I will look unto the LORD; I will wait for the God of my salvation: my God will hear me. Rejoice not against me, O mine enemy: when I fall, I shall arise; when I sit in darkness, the LORD shall be a light unto me. I will bear the indignation of the LORD, because I have sinned against him, until he plead my cause, and execute judgment for me: he will bring me forth to the light, and I shall behold his righteousness. (Micah 7:7–9)

With one mind, His guidance and direction may be heard—a majority elect drinking from the same fountain of advancing Bible light. Storms of conflict may arise, but glory from above will lift them above the world's "gravitational hold," that they may "fly" with relative ease, accelerating beyond the reach of waves of opposition. The harvest showers have been descending in small, scattered measures, but the reward of one rising generation of the remnant will be to enjoy God's outpouring without measure. "But they that wait upon the Lord shall renew their strength; they shall mount up with wings as eagles; they shall run, and not be weary; and they shall walk, and not faint" (Isa. 40:31).

Once the latter rain showers come down, there's no turning back. It is then that the last movements will be rapid ones, including the most massive counterassault ever conducted by well-entrenched powers of darkness. One passage that reflects and highlights final movement principles is Isaiah 30:15–31:5, which includes the following elements: returning/repentance, rest, trust, and grace (vs. 15, 18, 19); seeing (v. 20); hearing, following (v. 21); latter rain (v. 23); shaking (v. 28), and deliverance (vs. 4, 5).

God's yearning is to gather spiritual Elijah. They will cross the barrier and continue to New Jerusalem, where literal gates of pearl are opened. Then earth's makeover can commence in its time—Eden paradise restored.

We Are Well Able

Again, the Jordan River is within sight from the bank where we now stand, permitting us to say without hesitation, "it is an exceeding good land"; "Let us go up at once, and possess it; for we are well able to overcome it" (Numbers 14:7; 13:30). The day star is on the horizon.

Bibliography

Bauckham, Richard. *Jude–2 Peter, Volume 50*. Nashville, TN: Nelson/Word Publishing Group, 1983.

Coffman Commentary. StudyLight.org. http://1ref.us/ny (accessed 08/16/2018).

"Faster Than Sound: Secret History." Nova Online. http://1ref.us/nx (accessed 08/16/2018).

Frazee, W.D. *Another Arc to Build*.

Morneau, Roger J. *When You Need Incredible Answers to Prayer*. Hagerstown, MD: Review and Herald Publishing Association, 1995.

White, Ellen G. *The Acts of the Apostles*. Mountain View, CA: Pacific Press Publishing Association, 1911.

White, Ellen G. "Shall We Awake?" *Bible Training School*, November 1, 1911.

White, Ellen G. *Christ's Object Lessons*. Washington, DC: Review and Herald Publishing Association, 1900.

White, Ellen G. *Counsels on Diet and Foods*. Washington, DC: Review and Herald Publishing Association, 1938.

White, Ellen G. *The Desire of Ages*. Mountain View, CA: Pacific Press Publishing Association, 1898.

White, Ellen G. *Early Writings*. Washington, DC: Review and Herald Publishing Association, 1882.

White, Ellen G. Education. Mountain View, CA: Pacific Press Publishing Association, 1903.

White, Ellen G. The Ellen G. White 1888 Materials. Washington, DC: Ellen G. White Estate, 1987.

White, Ellen G. *Evangelism*. Washington, DC: Review and Herald Publishing Association, 1946.

White, Ellen G. *Gospel Workers*. Battle Creek, MI: Review and Herald Publishing Co., 1892.

White, Ellen G. *The Great Controversy*. Mountain View, CA: Pacific Press Publishing Association, 1911.

White, Ellen G. *Last Day Events*. Boise, ID: Pacific Press Publishing Association, 1992.

White, Ellen G. *Manuscript Releases*. Vol. 1. Silver Spring, MD: Ellen G. White Estate, 1981.

White, Ellen G. *Manuscript Releases*. Vol. 7. Silver Spring, MD: Ellen G. White Estate, 1990.

White, Ellen G. *Manuscript Releases*. Vol. 8. Silver Spring, MD: Ellen G. White Estate, 1990.

White, Ellen G. *Manuscript Releases*. Vol. 10. Silver Spring, MD: Ellen G. White Estate, 1990.

White, Ellen G. *Manuscript Releases*. Vol. 21. Silver Spring, MD: Ellen G. White Estate, 1993.

White, Ellen G. *Maranatha*. Washington, DC: Review and Herald Publishing Association, 1976.

White, Ellen G. *The Ministry of Healing*. Mountain View, CA: Pacific Press Publishing Association, 1905.

White, Ellen G. *My Life Today*. Washington, DC: Review and Herald Publishing Association, 1952.

White, Ellen G. "Offerings." *Pacific Union Recorder*, October 24, 1901.

White, Ellen G. *Patriarchs and Prophets*. Washington, DC: Review and Herald Publishing Association, 1890.

White, Ellen G. *Prophets and Kings*. Mountain View, CA: Pacific Press Publishing Association, 1917.

White, Ellen G. *The Publishing Ministry*. Hagerstown, MD: Review and Herald Publishing Association, 1983.

White, Ellen G. "Our Mighty Helper." *The Review and Herald*, July 1, 1884.

White, Ellen G. "Importance of Trust in God." *The Review and Herald*, May 10, 1887.

White, Ellen G. "Liberality the Fruit of Love." *The Review and Herald*, May 16, 1893.

White, Ellen G. "The Work Required of God's People." *The Review and Herald*, November 29, 1898.

White, Ellen G. "The Newcastle Camp-Meeting." *The Review and Herald*, April 11, 1899.

White, Ellen G. "Evidences of Discipleship." *The Review and Herald*, February 4, 1904.

White, Ellen G. "A Solemn Message to the Church." *The Review and Herald*, November 8, 1906.

White, Ellen G. "The Work in Oakland and San Francisco—No. 3." *The Review and Herald*, December 13, 1906.

White, Ellen G. "The World's Need." *The Review and Herald*, March 31, 1910.

White, Ellen G. "Go, Preach the Gospel." *The Review and Herald*, November 17, 1910.

White, Ellen G. *Selected Messages*. Book 1. Washington, DC: Review and Herald Publishing Association, 1958.

White, Ellen G. *Selected Messages*. Book 2. Washington, DC: Review and Herald Publishing Association, 1958.

White, Ellen G. *Selected Messages*. Book 3. Washington, DC: Review and Herald Publishing Association, 1980.

White, Ellen G. *Sermons and Talks*, Vol. 1. Silver Spring, MD: Ellen G. White Estate, 1990.

White, Ellen G. *Sermons and Talks*, Vol. 2. Silver Spring, MD: Ellen G. White Estate, 1994.

White, Ellen G. *The SDA Bible Commentary*. Vol. 4. Washington, DC: Review and Herald Publishing Association, 1955.

White, Ellen G. "The Christian's Hope." *The Signs of the Times*, May 29, 1884.

White, Ellen G. "Is Not This A Brand Plucked Out Of The Fire?" *The Signs of the Times*, June 2, 1890.

White, Ellen G. "The Crucifixion of Self." *The Signs of the Times*, April 9, 1902.

White, Ellen G. "The Lord's Prayer." *The Signs of the Times*, October 28, 1903.

White, Ellen G. *Sons and Daughters of God*. Washington, DC: Review and Herald Publishing Association, 1955.

White, Ellen G. *Steps to Christ*. Mountain View, CA: Pacific Press Publishing Association, 1892.

White, Ellen G. *The Story of Redemption*. Washington, DC: Review and Herald Publishing Association, 1947.

White, Ellen G. *Testimonies for the Church*. Vol. 1. Mountain View, CA: Pacific Press Publishing Association, 1868.

White, Ellen G. *Testimonies for the Church*. Vol. 2. Mountain View, CA: Pacific Press Publishing Association, 1871.

White, Ellen G. *Testimonies for the Church*. Vol. 4. Mountain View, CA: Pacific Press Publishing Association, 1881.

White, Ellen G. *Testimonies for the Church*. Vol. 5. Mountain View, CA: Pacific Press Publishing Association, 1889.

White, Ellen G. *Testimonies for the Church*. Vol. 6. Mountain View, CA: Pacific Press Publishing Association, 1901.

White, Ellen G. *Testimonies for the Church*. Vol. 8. Mountain View, CA: Pacific Press Publishing Association, 1904.

White, Ellen G. *Testimonies for the Church*. Vol. 9. Mountain View, CA: Pacific Press Publishing Association, 1909.

White, Ellen G. *Testimonies to Ministers and Gospel Workers*. Mountain View, CA: Pacific Press Publishing Association, 1923.

White, Ellen G. *That I May Know Him*. Washington, DC: Review and Herald Publishing Association, 1964.

White, Ellen G. *Thoughts from the Mount of Blessing*. Mountain View, CA: Pacific Press Publishing Association, 1896.

Wilson, Brian. "No Title." *Adventist Frontiers*, January 2005.

TEACH Services, Inc.
P U B L I S H I N G
www.TEACHServices.com • (800) 367-1844

We invite you to view the complete
selection of titles we publish at:
www.TEACHServices.com

We encourage you to write us
with your thoughts about this,
or any other book we publish at:
info@TEACHServices.com

TEACH Services' titles may be purchased in
bulk quantities for educational, fund-raising,
business, or promotional use.
bulksales@TEACHServices.com

Finally, if you are interested in seeing
your own book in print, please contact us at:
publishing@TEACHServices.com
We are happy to review your manuscript at no charge.

www.ingramcontent.com/pod-product-compliance
Lightning Source LLC
Chambersburg PA
CBHW071158160426
43196CB00011B/2123